Tokyo Subway System
東京地下鉄路線図

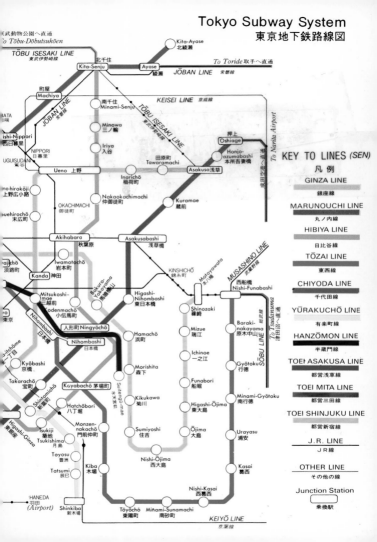

KEY TO LINES (SEN)
凡例

GINZA LINE
銀座線

MARUNOUCHI LINE
丸ノ内線

HIBIYA LINE
日比谷線

TŌZAI LINE
東西線

CHIYODA LINE
千代田線

YŪRAKUCHŌ LINE
有楽町線

HANZŌMON LINE
半蔵門線

TOEI ASAKUSA LINE
都営浅草線

TOEI MITA LINE
都営三田線

TOEI SHINJUKU LINE
都営新宿線

J.R. LINE
JR線

OTHER LINE
その他の線

Junction Station
乗換駅

TOKYO

A Pocket-Size

MAP English- Japanese

ポケット版 **東京2カ国語マップ**

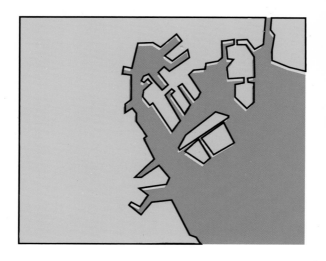

KASHIWASHOBO
柏書房

CONTENTS

TOKYO MAP

Published by Kashiwa Bijutsu Shupaan
Publishing Co., Ltd.
1-10-2-204 Mukōgaoka, Bunkyo-ku, Tokyo
113 Japan
Distribution by Kashiwashobo
Publishing Co., Ltd.
1-13-14 Honkomagome, Bunkyo-Ku,
Tokyo 113 Japan
Printed in Japan/First edition, 1992
by Toppan Printing Co., Ltd.
ISBN4-7601-0877-7

目　次

KEY　凡例

- Prefectural Boundary　都県界
- City *(-shi)* Boundary　市町界
- Ward *(-ku)* Boundary　区界
- Town *(-machi/-chō)* Boundary　町界
- J. R. Line　JR線
- Other Railway　その他の鉄道
- Subway　地下鉄
- Expressway　高速道路
- Ramp　高速道路ランプ
- (1) (2) (3)　Chōme Number　丁目番号
- Park　公園　Garden　庭園
- Government Office　官公庁　Embassy　外国公館
- Tourist Spot or Place of Historic Interest　名所旧跡
- Shintō Shrine (Shr.) *(Jinja)*　神社
- Buddhist Temple *(-ji, -in)*　寺院
- Church, Cathedral　教会
- Hospital (Hosp.)　病院
- School (Sch.)　学校

SAITAMA-KEN 埼玉県

CHICHIBU-TAMA NATIONAL PARK 秩父多摩国立公園

MEIJINOMORI-TAKAO QUASI-NAT'L PARK 明治の森高尾国定公園

YAMANASHI-KEN 山梨県

TANZAWA-ŌYAMA QUASI-NAT'L PARK 丹沢大山国定公園

KANAGAWA-KEN 神奈川県

FUJI-HAKONE-IZU NAT'L PARK 富士箱根伊豆国立公園

Nagatoro 長瀞
Yoshida 吉田
Ogano 小鹿野
Ōtaki 大滝
Mitsumineguchi 三峰口
Mitsumine-san 三峰山
Kumotori-yama 雲取山
Okutama 奥多摩
Otake-san 大岳山
Okanawachi 奥武蔵
Ōtsuki 大月
Ogiyama 扇山
Uenohara 上野原
Danpōzaka
TSURU 都留
Dōshi 道志
Tanzawa-yama 丹沢山
Ōyama 大山
Yabitsu 山北
Matsuda 松田
Miurazawa 三保沢
MINAMI-ASHIGARA 南足柄
GOTENBA 御殿場
Hakone-yama 箱根山
Ashinoko 芦ノ湖
Ranzan 嵐山
Ogawa 小川
Namegawa 滑川
HIGASHI-MATSUYAMA 東松山
Higashi-Matsuyama 東松山
Ogose 越生
Shōmaru-tōge 正丸峠
CHICHIBU 秩父
Buko-san 武甲山
HIDAKA 日高
HANNŌ 飯能
ŌME 青梅
IRUMA 入間
SAYAMA 狭山
HAMURA 羽村
AKIGAWA 秋川
FUSSA 福生
Itsukaichi 五日市
HACHIŌJI 八王子
Takao-san 高尾山
Tsukui 津久井
Tsukui-ko 津久井湖
HINODE 日の出
TACHIKAWA 立川
HIGASHI-YAMATO 東大和
HIGASHI-MURAYAMA 東村山
TOKOROZAWA 所沢
KIYOSE 清瀬
NIIZA 新座
KODAIRA 小平
KOGANEI 小金井
KOKUBUNJI 国分寺
FUCHŪ 府中
MITAKA 三鷹
MUSASHINO 武蔵野
CHŌFU 調布
Tokyo 東京
TAMA NEW TOWN 多摩ニュータウン
MACHIDA 町田
SAGAMIHARA 相模原
Shin-Yokohama 新横浜
ZAMA 座間
YAMATO 大和
AYASE 綾瀬
ATSUGI 厚木
ISEHARA 伊勢原
HADANO 秦野
Oi-Matsuda 大井松田
Nakai 中井
Hadano-Naka 秦野中井
HIRATSUKA 平塚
FUJISAWA 藤沢
Ōfuna 大船
KAMAKURA 鎌倉
Enoshima 江の島
ZUSHI 逗子
Hayama 葉山
CHIGASAKI 茅ヶ崎
Ōiso 大磯
Ninomiya 二宮
Kōzu 国府津
ODAWARA 小田原
Nakai 中井
Hakone 箱根

CHŪŌ EXPWY
KAN-ETSU EXPWY
TŌMEI EXPWY
YOKOHAMA LINE 横浜線
ŌDAKYŪ LINE 小田急線
SEIBU CHICHIBU LINE 西武秩父線
ŌME LINE 青梅線
CHŪŌ HONSEN 中央本線
TŌKAIDŌ SHINKANSEN 東海道新幹線
JŌETSU SHINKANSEN 上越新幹線

Sagami Wan (bay) 相模湾
Sagami-ko 相模湖
Odawara-Atsugi Dōro 小田原厚木道路
Seisho Bypass 西湘バイパス
Yokohama Shindō 横浜新道
Zuyō Shindō 逗葉新道

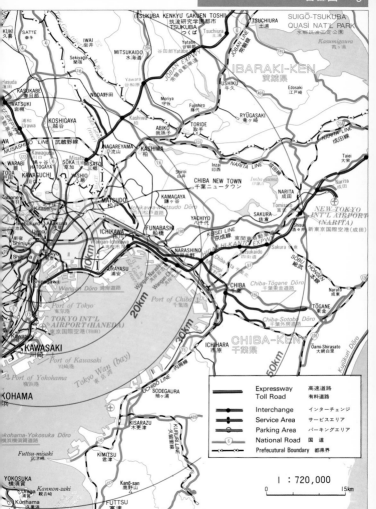

SUIGŌ-TSUKUBA QUASI NAT'L PARK
水郷筑波国定公園

IBARAKI-KEN
茨城県

CHIBA-KEN
千葉県

NEW TOKYO INT'L AIRPORT (NARITA)
新東京国際空港(成田)

TOKYO INT'L AIRPORT (HANEDA)
東京国際空港(羽田)

KAWASAKI
川崎

YOKOHAMA
横浜

	Expressway	高速道路
	Toll Road	有料道路
	Interchange	インターチェンジ
	Service Area	サービスエリア
	Parking Area	パーキングエリア
6	National Road	国道
	Prefectural Boundary	都県界

1 : 720,000

0 _____ 15km

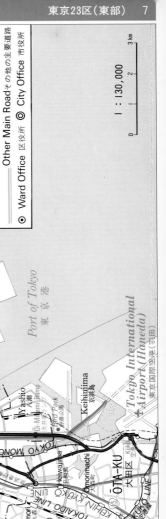

J.R. East Japan Line JR東日本線
Other Railway その他の鉄道
Expressway 高速道路
Shuto Expressway 首都高速道路
National Road 国道
Other Main Road その他の主要道路
I.C.インター
◉ Ward Office 区役所　◎ City Office 市役所

1 : 130,000

0　　　1　　　2　　　3 km

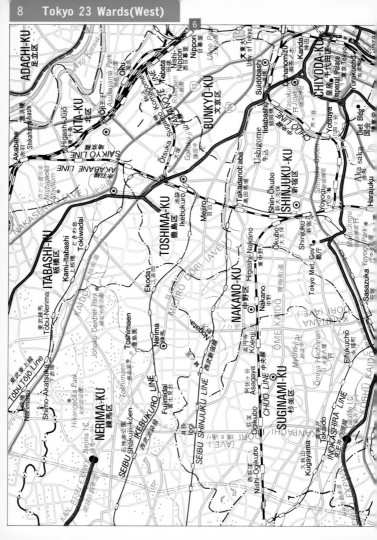

7

TOKYO TOWER
東京タワー

Mita
三田

Tamachi
田町

Shibaura
芝浦

Azabu
麻布

Shibuya
渋谷

Ebisu
恵比寿

YAMANOTE LINE
山手線

Naka-Meguro
中目黒

MEGURO-KU
目黒区

Meguro
目黒

Shimo-Kitazawa
下北沢

Sangenjaya
三軒茶屋

Musashi-Koyama
武蔵小山

Gakugei-Daigaku
学芸大学

Toritsu-Daigaku
都立大学

Jiyūgaoka
自由が丘

SETAGAYA-KU
世田谷区

SETAGAYA LINE

Kyōdō
経堂

Gotokuji
豪徳寺

Komazawa Olympic Park
駒沢オリンピック公園

Den-en-Chōfu
田園調布

Todoroki
等々力

ŌIMACHI LINE
大井町線

DEN-EN-CHŌFU DŌRI (AVE.)

TAMAGAWA DŌRI (AVE.)

ODAKYŪ LINE
小田急線

Shimo-Takaido
下高井戸

Sakurajōsui
桜上水

Kinuta Park
砧公園

Tokyu J.C.

Futako-Tamagawa
二子玉川

TAKATSU-KU
高津区

Kuji
久地

Musashi-Mizonokuchi
武蔵溝ノ口

Miyazakidai
宮崎台

Tama Gawa (R.)
多摩川

KAWASAKI CITY
川崎市

YOKOHAMA CITY
横浜市

Roka-Kōshun'en
芦花公園
蘆花恒春園

Seijō-Gakuen-mae
成城学園前

ŌI Futō (Wharf)
大井・ふ頭

Jūganochi Ramp

TOKYO MONO RAIL
東京モノレール

Shinagawa
品川

Ōi-machi
大井町

Nishi-Ōi
西大井

Ōsaki
大崎

Gotanda
五反田

Ōimachi
大井町

Ōmori
大森

TŌKAIDŌ LINE
東海道線

KEIHIN KYŪKŌ LINE
京浜急行線

Ōmorimachi
大森町

Keihinjima
京浜島

Heiwajima
平和島

SHINAGAWA-KU
品川区

Hatanodai
旗の台

MEKAMA LINE
目蒲線

ŌTA-KU
大田区

Honmon-ji
本門寺

Kamata
蒲田

Senzoku Pond
洗足池

Dōkanyama
道灌山

Senzoku Park
洗足公園

IKEGAMI LINE
池上線

YOKOSUKA LINE
横須賀線

TŌKAIDŌ SHINKANSEN
東海道新幹線

Kashimada
鹿島田

Hirama
平間

Mukaigawara
向河原

MEKAMA LINE
目蒲線

Musashi-Kosugi
武蔵小杉

NAKAHARA-KU
中原区

Musashi-Shinjō
武蔵新城

Musashi-Nakahara
武蔵中原

1 : 30,000

3 km

3 Km

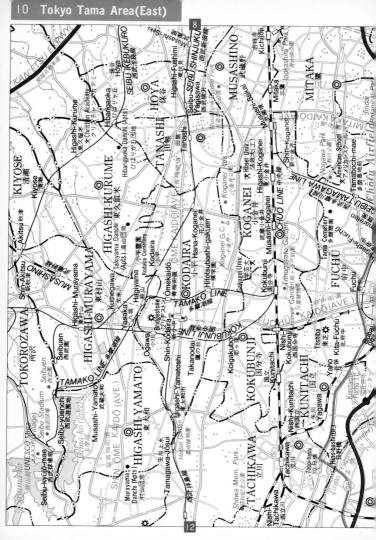

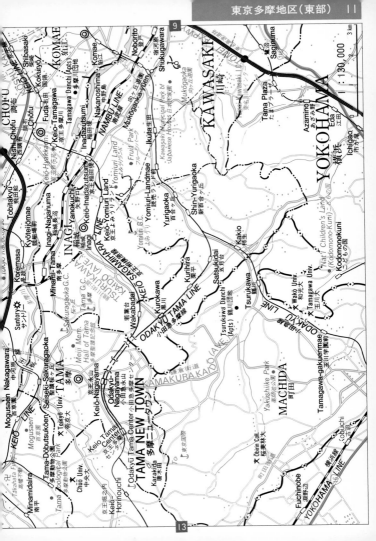

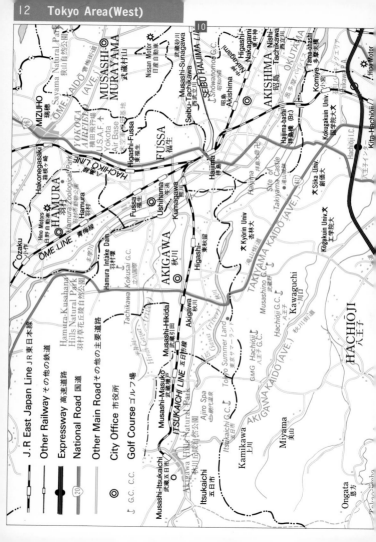

J.R East Japan Line JR東日本線

Other Railway その他の鉄道

Expressway 高速道路

National Road 国道

Other Main Road その他の主要道路

◎ City Office 市役所

⚑ G. C. C.C. Golf Course ゴルフ場

11

Toyoda 豊田

Hirayama-Jōshi-Kōen 平山城址公園
Naganuma 長沼
Kitano 北野
Hachiōji 八王子
Nishi-Hachiōji 西八王子
Katakura 片倉
Keiō-Katakura 京王片倉
Takao 高尾
Takaosanguchi 高尾山口

Musashino Mausoleum 武蔵野陵
Tama Mausoleum 多摩御陵
Tama Forest Science Garden 多摩森林科学園
Tokyo Univ. of Art and Design 東京造形大学
Site of Hachiōji Castle 八王子城址

Nippon Bunka Univ. 日本文化大学
Tokyo Engineering Coll. 東京工科大
Tokyo Met. Univ. 都立大学
Minami-Ōsawa 南大沢
Tama Univ. of Art 多摩美大

Tamasakai 多摩境
Hashimoto 橋本
Sagamihara 相模原
Minami-Hashimoto 南橋本
Kamimizo 上溝
Yabe 矢部
SAGAMIHARA 相模原
SAGAMI LINE 相模線

Mitsubishi Electric 三菱電機
Mitsubishi Heavy Ind. 三菱重工

MACHIDA KAIDŌ (AVE.) 町田街道
YOKOHAMA LINE 横浜線
CHŪŌ LINE 中央線
KEIŌ LINE 京王線
TAKAO LINE 高尾線
Hachiōji Bypass 八王子バイパス

Mejirodai めじろ台
Yamada 山田
Hazama 狭間

Sōbu G.C. 相武
Aihara 相原

Tokushuku Univ. 拓殖大
Tokyo Kasei Gakuin Coll. 東京家政学院大
Hōsei Univ. 法政大

Takao Mus. of Natural History 高尾自然科学博物館

SHIROYAMA 城山
Shiroyama-ko 城山湖
Shiroyama Dam 城山ダム
Sagami Gawa (river) 相模川

AKIRUNOMORI TAKAO QUASI-NATIONAL PARK 明治の森高尾国定公園

Takao-san 高尾山
Yaku-in 薬王院
Odarumi Pass 大垂水峠

Kobotoke Tunnel 小仏トンネル

KŌSHU KAIDŌ 甲州街道

Tsukuiko-ko 津久井湖
TSUKUI 津久井
Tsukuiko G.C. 津久井
相模湖ピクニックランド

I.C. Interchange インターチェンジ
P.A. Parking Area パーキングエリア

1 : 130,000

0　1　2　3 km

Ondacho
恩田町

Tsukushino
つくし野

AOBADAI AobadaI青葉台 DEN-EN TOSHI LINE
田園都市線

Nagatsuta
長津田

Ibukino
いぶき野

Nagatsutachō
長津田町

Tokyo Inst.
of Tech
東工大研究所

Kirigaoka
霧が丘

Fujigaoka
藤が丘

Fujisaki

港北P.A
Kohoku P.A

TOMEI EXPW 東名高速道路

Ichigaochō
市ケ尾町

KŌHOKU NEW TOWN
港北ニュータウン

Kita-Hassakuchō
北八朔町

Kawawachō
川和町

Tōkaichiba
十日市場

Tōkaichibachō
十日市場町 YOKOHAMA LINE 横浜線

Niiharuchō
新治町

MIDORI-KU
緑区

Nakayama
中山

Saedochō
佐江戸町

Katsutachō
勝田町

Higashiyamatachō
東方町

Ikenobechō
池辺町

Orimotochō
折本町

Dai Nippon Printing
大日本印刷

NEC
日本電気

Yamazaki Baking
山崎製パン

Katsu
港北

Matsushita
Communication
松下通信

YOKOHAMA I.C.
横浜インター

Wakabadai
若葉台

Kami-Kawaichō
上川井町

Kitamachi
北町

Citizen's Forest
市民の森

Midori Ward Office
緑区役所◉

Hikarigaoka Danchi (Apts)
ひかりが丘団地

Kawai-honchō
川井本町

Yukijirushi
雪印

Kamoi
鴨居

Myōyji
明星

Kami-Shiranechō
上白根町

Asahidai
旭台

Kamoichō
鴨居町

Takeyama
竹山

Higashi-Hongōchō
東本郷町

Kozu
小机

DAISAN KEIHIN

Sugatachō
菅田町

Hazawachō
羽沢町

HAZAWA
ON RAMP

U.S.Forces.
Signal Corps
米軍通信隊

Hodogaya G.C.
程ヶ谷ゴルフ場

ASAHI-KU
旭区

Imajuku
今宿

Tsuokachō
都岡町

YOKOHAMA CITY
横浜市

Shirane Fudo
白根不動

TOLL
GATE

SŌBU LINE

Seya Danchi (Apts)
瀬谷団地

Seyachō
瀬谷町

Seya
瀬谷

Mitsukyō
三ツ境

New Town Futamatagawa
ニュータウン二俣川

Sasanodai
笹野台

Tsurugamine
鶴ヶ峰

Asahi Ward Office
旭区役所◉

16

Nishiya
西谷

Kami-Hoshikawa
上星川

HODOGAYA I.C.

Yokohama Nat'l Univ.
横浜国大

Mitsu

Seya Ward Office
瀬谷区役所◉

SEYA-KU
瀬谷区

Kibogaoka
希望が丘

Akuwachō
阿久和町

Shimo-Seya
下瀬谷

Futamatagawa
二俣川

Prefectural Hygiene Jr. Coll.
県立衛生短大

相模鉄道

Makigahara
万騎が原

Minami-
Makigahara
南万騎が原

Sakonyama
左近山

Ichizawa
市沢

Wadamachi
和田町

HODOGAYA-KU
保土ケ谷区

Hodogaya Park
保土ケ谷公園

Pref.
Nutrition Coll.
県立栄養短大

Hodogaya
保土ケ谷

TOKAIDO-SANYO SHINKANSEN
東海道・山陽新幹線

IZUMINO LINE 相鉄いずみ野線

Totsuka C.C.
戸塚カントリークラブ

Yokohama C.C.
横浜カントリークラブ

TOTSUKA-KU
戸塚区

Kawakamichō
川上町

HODOGAYA
BYPASS

SHIN-HODOGAYA
I.C.

Hodogaya
程ケ谷

TOKAIDO MAIN LINE 東海道本線

Kami-Iidachō
上飯田町

Izumino
いずみ野

Izumichō
和泉町

Yayoidai
弥生台

Okazuchō
岡津町

Ryokuen-toshi
緑園都市

Nasechō
名瀬町

Makigahara
万騎が原

Kami-Yabechō
上矢部町

Akibachō
秋葉町

Higashi-
Totsuka
東戸塚

Hiradochō
平戸町

TOLL GATE

Idogaya
井土ケ谷

MINAMI
南

Gumyōji
弘明寺

Gumyōji
弘明寺

IZUMI-KU
泉区

Shimo-Iidachō
下飯田町

Nakadachō
中田町

Yabechō
矢部町

Kashiochō
柏尾町

Shimo-Nagayachō
下永谷町

KONAN-KU
港南区

Bridgestone
ブリヂストン

Hitachi 日立

KŌHOKU-KU
港北区
n-Yoshidachō
新吉田町　Tsunashima
綱島温泉
Tsunashima
綱島
Komaokachō
駒岡町

Yumenogasaki
Park 夢見ケ崎公園
Yako 矢向

Shitte 尻手

SAIWAI-KU
幸区

Rokugō-bashi (Br.)
六郷橋

DAISHI LINE 大師線
Kawasaki-Daishi
川崎大師

syama Japanese
d Garden
富山梅林
pachō
羽口町　Okurayama
大倉山

Meiji Seika Central Research Lab.
明治製菓中央研究所

Mitsuike Park
三ツ池公園

Shishigayachō
獅子ケ谷町

Sueyoshi
末吉

Morinaga (Confec.)
森永製菓

Tsurumi-
Ichiba
鶴見市場

City Office
市役所

KAWASAKI-KU
川崎区

Hatchōnawate
八丁畷

Kawasaki-Shinmachi
川崎新町

YOKOHAMA
横浜

KAWASAKI CITY
川崎市

Hama-Kawasaki
浜川崎

Kita-Terao
北寺尾　Baba-
馬場

Shin-Yokohama
新横浜

Kikuna
菊名

Shinohara
篠原

Myōrenji
妙蓮寺

TSURUMI-KU
鶴見区

Sōjiji (temple)
総持寺

Tsurumi
鶴見

Tsurumi Ward Office
鶴見区役所

Kokudo
国道

Tsurumi-Ono
鶴見小野

Shōwa
昭和

Ōgimachi
扇町

Musashi-Shiraishi
武蔵白石

Anzen
安善

Asano
浅野

Shin-
Shibaura
新芝浦

Okawa
大川

Anzen
安善

NAGAWAKU
神奈川区

Kanagawa Univ
神奈川大学

Yokohama Coll.
of Commerce
横浜商科大学

Oguchi
大口

Hakuraku
白楽

Shin-Koyasu
新子安

Koyasu
子安

Kanagawa-
Shinmachi
神奈川新町

Nakakido
仲木戸

Higashi-Kanagawa
東神奈川

Nissan Motor
日産自動車

Umi-Shibaura
海芝浦

Tōshiba Turbin
東芝タービン

Yokohama Thermoelectric Power Plant
東電横浜火力発電所

Ōgishima
扇島

NKK Ōgishima
NKK扇島工場

扇島火力発電所

Daikoku-Ōhashi (Br.)
大黒大橋

Mizuho Futō
瑞穂ふ頭
(wharf)

Daikoku Futō (wharf)
大黒ふ頭

Daikoku I.C.
大黒インター

Port of Yokohama
横浜港

94

Yokohama Bay Bridge
横浜ベイブリッジ

SHI-KU
西区

Sakuragichō
桜木町

Prefectural
Office 県庁

City Office
市役所

Yamashita-chō
山下町

Kanno
関内

Ishikawachō
石川町

Motomachi
元町

Minatonomieruoka Park
港の見える丘公園

Honmoku Futō (wharf)
本牧ふ頭

Yamatechō
山手町

Yamate Police Sta.
山手警察

Yamate
山手

NAKA-KU
中区

Negishi Cemetery
根岸共同墓地

Honmokuchō
本牧町

Nissan Motor Wharf
日産自動車専用埠頭

Mitsubishi Heavy Industries
三菱重工業

Honmoku Sea-fishing facilities
本牧海づり施設

Negishi Forest Park
根岸森林公園

Santonodai Prehistoric Site

Makadochō
間門町

Sankei-en (garden)
三渓園

SOGO-KU
磯子区

Negishi
根岸

NEGISHI LINE 根岸線

Honmoku Citizen's Park
本牧市民公園

Tokyo Gas

Isogo Thermoelectric
Power Plant 磯子火力発電所

Nippon Petrochemical
日本石油化学

1 : 173,000

0 _____ 4 km

Toneri
舎人

SŌKA CITY
草加市

Kojiyachō
古千谷町

Iriyachō
入谷町
Iriya 入谷
Kojiya
古千谷
Tonerichō
舎人町

Higashi-Ikōchō
東伊興町

Adachi Distribution Center
足立流通センター

Hōtori Jinja (Shr.)
大鷲神社

Hanahata Danchi
(Apts)花畑団地

Yashio-mini
八潮ミニ

Iryachō

Ikō
伊興

Nishi-Hokima
西保木間

Hanahata
花畑

Shinmei
神明

Kaga
加賀

Nishi-Ikō
西伊興

Takenotsuka
竹ノ塚

Hokima
保木間

Fuchie H. Sch.
淵江高

Minami-Hanahata
南花畑

Shinmei-minami
神明南

Yazaike
谷在家

Adachi Tech. H. Sch.
足立工業高校

Takeno-tsuka
竹の塚

Higashi-Hokima
東保木間

Kita-Kaheichō
北加平町

Rokugatsu
六月

Higashi-Rokuga-tsuchō
東六月町

Hotsukachō
保塚町

Rokuchō
六町

Enten-ji 卍

ADACHI-KU
足立区

Nishiarai
西新井

Kurihara
栗原

Shimane
島根

Hirano
平野

Hitotsuya
一ツ家

Nishi-Kahei
西加平

Kahei Yanaka
加平 谷中

Nishiarai Daishi
西新井大師

Daishi-mae 卍

Kita-

adachi-Nishi
H. Sch.
足立西高

Nishiarai-Honchō
西新井本町

Nishiarai
西新井

Umejima
梅島

Chūō-Honchō
中央本町

Kahei Ramp.
加平ランプ

Nishiarai-Sakaechō
西新井栄町

Umejima
梅島

Aoi
青井

Kōhoku
江北

Okino
興野

Sekihara
関原

Adachi H. Sch.
足立高校

Aoi H. Sch.
青井高校

Kōdō
弘道

Higashi-Ayase
東綾瀬

Ōgi
扇

Umeda
梅田

Gotanno
五反野

Nishi-Ayase
西綾瀬

Ayase
綾瀬

Motoki
本木

KAWAGUCHI LINE

Adachi
足立

Nishi-Kame
西亀

SHUTO EX

Senju-shinbashi (Br.)
千住新橋

Tokyo Prison
東京拘置所

Ogi-ōhashi (Br.)
扇大橋

Nishiarai-bashi (Br.)
西新井橋

Senju-Ōkawachō
千住大川町

Kosuge
小菅

Kosuge
小菅

Katsushik

Higas Horiki
東堀切

Otake-bashi (Br.)
尾竹橋

Senju
千住

Hinodechō
日ノ出町

Kosuge I.C.

Kita-Senju
北千住

ARAKAWA-KU
荒川区

Adachi Ward Office
足立区役所

Yanagihara
柳原

Ushida
牛田

Horikiri-bashi (Br.)
堀切橋

Horikiri-Shōbuen
堀切菖蒲園

Horikiri
堀切

Takar mach
宝町

KEISEI MAIN LIN

Machiya
町屋

Senju-Ōhashi
千住大橋

Keisei-Sekiya
京成関屋

Horikin Shōbben
堀切菖蒲園

Yotsugi
四ツ木

Shin-Mikawashima
新三河島

Arakawa Ward Office
荒川区役所

Tsutsumidōri Ramp
堤通ランプ

Mikawashima
三河島

Minami-Senju
南千住

Kanegafuchi
鐘ヶ淵

1 : 70,000
0　　　　　　　1　　　　　　　2 km

MATSUDO
CITY
松戸市

SHIO CITY
八潮市

MISATO CITY
三郷市

MATSUDO BASHI TOLL ROAD

Kita-Matsudo
北松戸

Yashio Ramp
八潮ランプ

Higashi-Mizumoto
東水元

Mizumoto Park
水元公園

Mizumoto-kōen
水元公園

Nishi-Mizumoto
西水元

Mizumoto
水元

Matsudo
松戸

MATSUDO CITY
松戸市

i-higashi H. Sch.
高

Mizumoto
水元
H. Sch.
水元高校

Katori Jinja
香取神社

Honjo Tech. H. Sch.
本所工業高校

Katsushika-
ōhashi (Br.)
葛飾大橋

Katsushika-bashi (Br.)
葛飾橋

agawa Park
中川公園

Minami-
Mizumoto
南水元

Handa Inari
半田稲荷

Nakagawa
中川

Mitsubishi Paper
三菱製紙

Higashi-Kanamachi
東金町

Kasai Jinja
葛西神社

Nijusseikigaoka
二十世紀ヶ丘

Kanamachi
金町

MITO KAIDO (AVE.)　水戸街道

JŌBAN LINE
常磐線

Kameari
亀有

Keisei-
Kanamachi
京成金町

Shin-Katsushika-bashi (Br.)
新葛飾橋

n H. Sch.
高

Niijuku
新宿

Kanamachi
金町

Yagiri　矢切

Kanamachi Filtration Plant
金町浄水場

Ūtoku Gakuen
修徳学園

Katsushika Comm. H. Sch.
葛飾商業高校

Shibamata
柴又

Shibamata Taishakuten
帝釈天

Yagirino-watashi
矢切の渡し

TSUSHIKA-KU
irotori 葛飾区

Shibamata
柴又

Edo Gawa (River)　江戸川

白鳥

Technoplaza Katsushika
テクノプラザかつしか

Kamakura
鎌倉

Aoto
青戸 Aoto
青砥

Takasago
高砂

KEISEI MAIN LINE
京成本線

Keisei-Takasago
京成高砂

本所
Ward Office
Tateishi
立石

Hosoda
細田

Aikoku Gakuen
愛国学園

Keisei-Koiwa
京成小岩

Kita-Koiwa
北小岩

Kōnodai Park
国際合公園

Chiba Univ.
千葉大

AGE
上野
Higashi-Tateishi
東立石

KAN-NANA DORI (AVE.)

Nishi-Koiwa
西小岩

Okudo
奥戸

国府台
Kōnodai

Ichikawa
市川

Mama
真間

Edogawa

Koiwa　小岩

6

Tateishi
立石

Ikebukuro
池袋

Ueno
上野

Shinjuku
新宿

Tokyo
東京

Shibuya
渋谷

MEIJI DORI (AVE.)
Minowa
明治通り

16

Sumida
墨田

Yotsugi-bashi
四ツ木橋

Nippori
日暮里

Sendagi
千駄木

Uguisudani
鶯谷

Higashi-
Mukōjima
東向島
Higashi-Mukōjima
東向島

Arakawa
荒川

Kinega
木根川

Hikifune
曳舟

Yahiro
八広

Higashi
Sumida
東墨田

Nezu
根津

Ueno Park
上野公園

TAITŌ-KU
台東区
Asakusa
浅草

Mukōjima
向島

Kyōjima
京島

Keisei-Hikifune
京成曳船

Univ. of Tokyo
東京大学

Ueno
上野

Sensō-ji
浅草寺

Narihirabashi
業平橋

Oshiage
押上

Omurai
小村井

Tachiban
立花

Yushima

Ueno Ramp

Asakusa
浅草

Bunka
文花

Kao
花王

Higashi
Azuma
あずま

Kuramae
蔵前

Sumida Ward Office
墨田区役所
Komagata Ramp

Narihira
業平

Yokokawa
横川

Hagi-dera
萩寺

Kōtō Comm
江東商業

Okachimachi

Honjo 本所

Kameido Tenjin
(Shr.) 亀戸天神

Akihabara
秋葉原

Ishiwara
石原

SUMIDA-KU 墨田区

Seikosha
精工舎

Kameido-Suijin
亀戸水神

Kuramae

Asakusabashi
浅草橋

Kakugikan

Kamezawa 亀沢

Kinshichō
錦糸町

Kameido
亀戸

Kanda
神田

Ryōgoku
両国

Ryōgoku H. Sch.
両国高

Kinshichō Ramp

Kameido
亀戸

14

Nihombashi
日本橋

Midori
緑

Tatekawa
立川

Mōri
毛利

Sarue Park
猿江公園

Jōtō H. Sch.
城東高校

SHUTO EXPW

Kanda
神田

23

Edobashi I.C.

Morishita

Kikukawa
菊川

Sumiyoshi
住吉

Nishi-Ojima
西大島

Suitengū-mae

Tōkyō City Air Terminal
東京シティエアー
ターミナル

Shirakawa
白河

Kiyosumi Garden
清澄庭園

Ōgibashi 扇橋

Kita-Suna
北砂

TOKYO

Kiyozumi Ramp

Hirano
平野

Sengoku
千石

Minami-
南砂

KŌTŌ-KU 江東区

CHŪŌ-KU
中央区

Monzen-
Nakachō

Tōyō
東陽

Kōtō Ward
Office
江東区役所

Ginza
銀座

Chūō Ward Office
中央区役所

Etchūjima
越中島

Kiba Ramp

Toyocho
東陽町

TOZAI LINE

Tsukuda
佃

Tsukiji

Tokyo Univ. of
Mercantile Marine
東京商船大学

Fukagawa Danchi (Apts)
深川団地

Shin-Suna
新砂

New Tokyo P.O.

Tsukishima
月島

Toyosu
豊洲

Shiomi
潮見

新東京局

Central Wholesale Market
中央卸売市場

Kachidoki
勝どき

Ishikawajima-Harima
石川島播磨

Shiomi
潮見

Timber dock
貯木場

Harumi
晴海

Toyosu
豊洲

Tatsumi
辰巳

Yumenoshim

Harumi
晴海

1 : 70,000

Tatsumi Danchi
(Apts) 辰巳団地

Shinonome
東雲

Yumenoshima Park
夢の島公園

0   2 km

Tatsumi I.C.

17

森永乳業 Morinaga Milk

Heiwa-bashi 平和橋

Higashi-Shin-Koiwa 東新小岩

Nishi-Shin-Koiwa 西新小岩

聖徳栄養短大 Seitoku Nutrition Jr. Coll. (Br.)

Hirai-Ōhashi 平井大橋

Shin-Koiwa 新小岩

小岩高校 Koiwa H. Sch.

Hon-Isshiki 本一色

Shin-Koiwa 新小岩

Matsushima 松島

NOBU MAIN LINE 総武本線

Kantō Daiichi H. Sch. 関東第一高校

Edogawa H. Sch. 江戸川高校

Komatsugawa-bashi (Br.) 小松川橋

Hirai 平井

Nishi-Komatsugawamachi 西小松川町

Komatsugawa Ramp 小松川

Arakawa-ōhashi (Br.) 荒川大橋

Komatsugawa 小松川

Higashi-Komatsugawa 東小松川

Funabori-bashi (Br.) 船堀橋

igashi-Ojima

ashi-una

Ara-kawa (river) 荒川

NJUKU LINE

Minami-Koiwa 南小岩

CHIBA KAIDO (AVE.) 千葉街道

Matsumoto-chō 松本町

Matsumoto 松本

Shishibone 鹿骨

Ōsugi 大杉

Chūō 中央

Edogawa Ward Office 江戸川区役所

Niihori 新堀

Nishi-Komatsugawamachi 西小松川町

EDOGAWA-KU 江戸川区

Nishi-Ichinoe 西一之江

Matsue 松江

Ichinoe 一之江

Ichinoe Ramp

Higashi-Koiwa 東小岩

Ichikawa 市川

Shinden 新田

Kita-Shinozakimachi 北篠崎町

Shinozaki Park 篠崎公園

Kami-Shinozakimachi 上篠崎町

Shinozaki 篠崎

KEIYO DORO AVE. 京葉道路

Shinozakimachi 篠崎町

Yagōchimachi 谷河内町

篠崎高校 Shinozaki H. Sch.

Minami-Shinozakimachi 南篠崎町

Higashi-Shinozakimachi 東篠崎町

Nishi-Mizue 西瑞江

Higashi-Mizue 東瑞江

Edogawa 江戸川

Mizue-Ōhashi (Br.) 瑞江大橋

Imai-bashi (Br.) 今井橋

ICHIKAWA CITY 市川市

Ichinoechō 一之江

Kasai Tech. H. Sch. 葛西工高

Funabori 船堀

Haruechō 春江町

Mizuho-Ōhashi (Br.) 瑞穂大橋

Ukitachō 宇喜田町

Kita-Kasai 北葛西

Edogawa 江戸川

Edo-gawa (river) 江戸川

GYOYOKU LOOP

KASAIBASHI DORI (AVE.) 葛西橋通り

Nishi-Kasai 西葛西

Urayasu-bashi (Br.) 浦安橋

EXPWY CHŪŌ LOOP 中央環状

Sewage nt 処理場

Seishinchō 清新町

Nishi-Kasai 西葛西

Naka-Kasai 中葛西

Higashi-Kasai 東葛西

Kasai-bashi (Br.) 葛西橋

Kasai-minami H. Sch. 葛西南高

Sewage Disposal Plant 下水処理場

Nihon Roll 日本ロール

Minami-Kasai 南葛西

va-Wangan-bashi 荒川湾岸橋 (Br.)

Rinkaichō 臨海町

Ichikawa

Ikebukuro 池袋

Shinjuku 新宿

Shibuya 渋谷

Ueno 上野

Tokyo 東京

1 : 70,000

0 1 2 km

Daito Bunka Univ.
大東文化大学

Daimon
卍 大門

Tokyo Daibutsu
東京大仏

Nat'l Saitama Hosp.
国立埼玉病院

Eidan-Narimasu
営団成増

Narimasu
成増

Yotsuba
四葉

ITABASHI-KU
板橋区

Akatsuka
赤塚

Tokumaru
徳丸

Nishidai
西台

西台 Nakadai Ramp
中台ランプ

Sun City サンシティ

Nakadai
中台

Akatsuka-shinmachi
赤塚新町

Shimo-Akatsuka
下赤塚

東武練馬
Tōbu-Nerima

Wakagi
若木

Kami-Itabas
上板橋

Hasune
蓮根

Aioichō
相生町

SHUTO E

Sakas

Hikarigaoka Park
光が丘公園

Eidan-Akatsuka
営団赤塚

254

Kitamachi
北町

TŌBU TŌJŌ LINE
東武東上

Nishiki
錦

Sakuragawa
桜川

Hikarigaoka Park Town
光が丘パークタウン

Doshida
土支田

Hikarigaoka
光が丘

Tagara
田柄

Heiwadai
平和台

Nishiki
錦

Jōhoku Central Park
城北中央公園

Hikawadai
氷川台

Komone
小茂根

Nerima I.C.
練馬インター

NERIMA-KU
練馬区

Yahara
谷原

Takamatsu
高松

Kasugachō
春日町

Hayamiya
早宮

CAN-NANA

Hazawa
羽沢

Shin-Sakuradai
新桜台

Kotakechō
小竹町

Mukaih

MEJIRO DŌRI (AVE.)

Takanodai
高野台

Chōmei-Ji
長命寺

Toshimaen
豊島園

Sakuradai
桜台

Musashino Academia Musicae
武蔵野音楽大学

Fujimidai
富士見台

Nukui
貫井

Kōyama
向山

Toshimaen
豊島園

Nerima
練馬

Sakuradai
桜台

Ekoda
江古田

Nihon Un
日本大

(Art)日大う

Minamitanaka
南田中

Nakamurabashi
中村橋

Nerima Ward Office
練馬区役所

Toyotama-Kita
豊玉北

Nerima 練馬

14 桜台

Musashi Univ.
武蔵大学

Asahigaoka
旭丘

Santa Maria Sch.
サンタマリアスクール

Fujimidai
富士見台

Nakamura
中村

MEJIRO DŌRI (AVE.)

Hig

Ikuei Tech Coll.
育英工業高専

Kami-Saginomiya
上鷺宮

Nakamura-minami
中村南

Toyotama-naka
豊玉中

Eharachō
江原町

Egota
江古田

Nishi-Oc

Igusa
井草

Iogi 井荻

Shimo-Igusa
下井草

Saginomiya
鷺宮

Saginomiya
鷺ノ宮

Toyotama-minami
豊玉南

Numabukuro
沼袋

Nat'l Nakano Hosp.
国立中野病院

Kokusai Jr. Coll.
国際短大

Matsugaoka
松が丘

Tetsugakudo

SEIBU SHINJUKU LINE 西武新宿線

Shimo-Igusa
下井草

Shirasagi
白鷺

Tojitsu-Kasei
都立家政

Maruyama
丸山

Nogata
野方

Numabukuro
沼袋

WASEDA DŌRI (AVE.)

Myōshō-Ji
妙正寺

Wakamiya
若宮

Nogata
野方

Arai-Yakushi
新井薬師前

Arai-Yakushi
新井薬師

Kami-Takada
上高田

Shimizu
清水

Hon-Amanuma
本天沼

Yamatochō
大和町

NAKANO-KU
中野区

Arai
新井

CHŪŌ DŌRI
中野サンプラザ

Suginami Public Hall
杉並公会堂

Amanuma
天沼

Asagaya-Kita
阿佐谷北

Kawakita Hosp.
河北病院

Kōenji-Kita
高円寺北

Nakano Sun Plaza 上高田

Nakano Ward Office
中野区役所

Nakano Culture Center
中野区文化センタ

Minami-Ogikubo

Ogikubo
荻窪

Asagaya-Minami
阿佐谷南

Asagaya 阿佐ヶ谷

Kōenji
高円寺

Kōenji-Minami
高円寺南

Suginami Ward Office
杉並区役所

Nakano
中野

Nakano
中野

Umewaka Noh Theater
梅若能楽堂

Minami-Ogikubo
荻窪 Minami-Asagaya

Chūō 中央

22

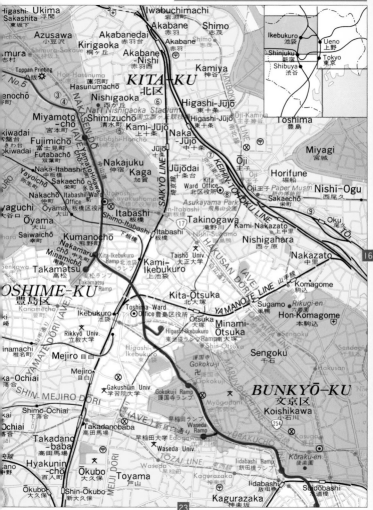

20

Suginami Ward Office 杉並区役所

MARUNOUCHI LINE

Chūo 中央 Nakano Sakai

Umezato 梅里

Shin-Kōenji 新高円寺 Higashi-Kōenji 東高円寺 Shin-Nakano 新中野 Honchō 本町

Narita-Higashi 成田東

Myōhō-ji 妙法寺 Rissho-Kōseikai 立正佼成会 Nakano-Fujimichō 中野富士見町 Nakano-Shimbashi 中野新橋

Horinouchi 堀ノ内

Wada 和田

Yayoichō 弥生町

Matsunoki 松ノ木

Takachiho Coll. of Commerce 高千穂商科大学

Omiya 大宮 Omiya Hachiman 大宮八幡

Honanchō 方南町

Minamidai 南台 Honmac 本町

Hamadayama 浜田山

Nishi-Eifuku 西永福

Daien-ji 大円寺 Kama-dera 蚕糸

Izumi 和泉 Kumano Jinja 熊野神社

Hōnan 方南 Hatagaya Ramp 幡ヶ谷ランプ Hatagaya

Eifukuchō 永福町

Daitabashi 代田橋 Nishihar 西原

Takaido Ramp 高井戸ランプ

Shimo-Takaido 下高井戸 Eifuku 永福 Meiji Univ 明治大学 Eifuku Ramp 永福ランプ

Hachimanyama 八幡山

KEIŌ LINE 京王線 Ōhara 大原

Sasazuka 笹塚 Yo

Kami-Kitazawa 上北沢 Ōyamacho 大山町 Yo Ueh

Roka-koshun-en 芦花公園 Sakurajōsui 桜上水 Shimo-Takaido 下高井戸 Meidaimae 明大前 Higashi-Kitazawa 東北沢 Nihon Minge 日本民芸

Hachiman-yama 八幡山 Nihon Univ. 日本大学（文理） Matsubara 松原 Shin-Daita 新代田 INOKASHIRA LINE 井の頭線

Sakurajōsui 桜上水 Matsubara 松原 Hanegi 羽根木 Shimo-Kita 下北沢 Ikenoue 池ノ上 Tokyo M 東京

Keisen-jogakuen (Sch.) 恵泉女学園 Akatsutsumi 赤堤 Daita 代田 Kokusai H.S. 国際高 都立国際

Chitosedai 千歳台 Funabashi 船橋 Yamashita 山下 Umegaoka 梅ヶ丘 Setagaya-Daita 世田谷代田 Daizawa 代沢 Ikejir

Chitosegaoka H. Sch. 千歳丘高校 Kyōdō 経堂 Gōtokuji 豪徳寺 Kokushikan Univ. 国士舘大学 Nat'l Children's Hosp 国立小児病院 Mishuku 三宿

Chitose-Funabashi 千歳船橋 ODAKYU LINE 小田急線 Miyasaka 宮坂 Setagaya Ward Office 世田谷区役所 Wakabayashi 若林 Taishidō 太子堂 Shōwa Wome 昭和女子

SETAGAYA-KU 世田谷区 Miyanosaka 宮の坂 Kamimachi 上町 Setagaya 世田谷 Shōin-jinjamae 松陰神社前 SETAGAYA LINE Sang 三軒 Setaga

Soshigaya-Okura 祖師ヶ谷大蔵 Sakura 桜 Shimour 下馬

Sakuragaoka 桜丘 Tokyo Univ. of Agri. 東京農業大学 Setagaya Magistrate's Residence (Setagaya Daikan Yashiki) 代官屋敷 Meiji Coll. of Pharm. 明治薬科大学 Nihon Univ. (Vetr 日本大学（農獣医）

Kinuta 砧 Baji Kōen (park) 馬事公苑 Tsurumaki 弦巻 Kamiuma 上馬 Nozawa 野沢 Gakugei-Univ. 学芸大学

Kantō Chūo Hosp. 関東中央病院 Komazawa Daigaku 駒沢大学 Higashiga-oka 東が丘

Kami-Yōga 上用賀 Sakura-Shinmachi 桜新町 Komazawa Univ. 駒沢大学 Nat'l Tokyo No.2 Hosp. 国立東京第二病院

Nat'l Okura Hosp. 国立大蔵病院 Komazawa Olympic Park 駒沢オリンピック公園 Yagumo 八雲 Kakinokizaka 柿の木坂

Okura 大蔵 Kinuta Park 砧公園 Yōga 用賀 Setagaya Tokyo I.C. 東京I.C.

Okamoto 岡本 Tamagawa-dai H.S. 玉川高校 Fukazawa H. Sch. 深沢高校 TOKYO

Seikado Library 静嘉堂文庫 Kinuta Tech. H. Sch. 砧工業高校 Seta 瀬田 Seisen Int'l Sch. 清泉インターナショナル学園 Nippon Coll. of Health & P.E. 日本体育大学 Engei H. Sch. 園芸高校 Fukazawa 深沢 Toritsu-Daigaku 都立大学 Taira mach

TAMAGAWA

DORI AVE.

Nakamachi 中町

1 : 70,000

0 2 km

24

21

Kagurazaka
神楽坂

Seibu-Shinjuku
西武新宿
Kabuki-
chō
歌舞伎町
SHINJUKU-KU
新宿区
Ichigaya
市ヶ谷

Yasukuni Jinja
靖国神社

Shinjuku
新宿

yō Met. Gov't
都庁
hi-Shinjuku
西新宿

TOEI SHINJUKU LINE

Ichigaya
市ヶ谷

CHIYODA-KU
千代田区

Shinjuku
新宿

Yotsuya
四谷

Kōjimachi
麹町

Imperial Palace
皇居

20
Ramp

Yoyogi
代々木

Shinjuku Gyoen
新宿御苑
Yoyogi
代々木

Yotsuya
四ツ谷

ODAKYU LINE

SHUTO

Sendagaya
千駄ヶ谷
Shinanomachi
信濃町

State Guesthouse
迎賓館

DIET BUILDING
国会議事堂

EXPWY No.4
首都高速4号線

Meiji Jingū
明治神宮

Meiji Jingū Outer Gardens
明治神宮外苑

Kasumigaseki
霞が関
Nagatacho
永田町

渋谷区

Kita-Aoyama
北青山

Aoyama-Ichome
青山一丁目

ara

Yoyogi Park
代々木公園

Harajuku
原宿

Jingūmae
神宮前

Minami-
Aoyama
南青山

Akasaka
赤坂

GINZA

Shimbashi
新橋

1

Yoyogi-kōen
代々木公園

Omotesando

Roppongi
六本木

246

CHIYODA LINE

Kamiyachō
神谷町

sm
NHK

Tokyo Tower
東京タワー

18

Tokyo
大学 (教育)
aba-Todaimae

Shibuya
渋谷

MINATO-KU
港区

Zōjō-ji
増上寺

15

Shinsen
神泉

Ichinohashi
一ノ橋

ashi

NY

Aobadai
青葉台

SHIBUYA-KU
渋谷区

Azabu
麻布

Hiro-o

Mita
三田

Keio Univ.
慶応大学

Mita

ashiyama
東山

代官山

Ebisu
恵比寿

HIBIYA LINE

EXPWY No.2

Tengenji Ramp

Tamachi
田町

Naka-Meguro
中目黒

Kami-Meguro
上目黒

三田
Mita

Shirokane
白金

MONORAIL

tenji
寺

Naka-Meguro
中目黒

Nat'l Park for
Nature Study
国立自然教育園

Sengakuji
泉岳寺

Chūōchō
中央町
Nakachō
中町

Meguro
目黒
Meguro
目黒

Shinagawa
品川

Shinagawa Futō (Wharf)
品川ふ頭

Meguro Ward Office
目黒区役所

MEGURO-KU
目黒区

kaban

Meguro-
Honcho
目黒本町

Meguro Fudō
目黒不動
Fudōmae
不動前

Gotanda
五反田

1

Ōsaki
大崎

15

Kita-Shinagawa
北品川

Rinshino-mori Park
林試の森公園

onya

Musashi-Koyama
武蔵小山

Ebara Ramp

Hoshi Coll. of Pharm
星薬科大学

Ōsaki
大崎

Shin-Banba
新馬場

Haramachi
原町

Nishi-Koyama
西小山

Togoshi-Ginza
戸越銀座

Togoshi Ramp

Togoshi
戸越

25

Tamagawa-dai 玉川台

Seta 瀬田

Tamagawa 玉川

Komazawa Olympic Park 駒沢オリンピック公園

Fukazawa 深沢 H. Sch 深沢高校

Seisen Int'l Sch. 清泉インターナショナル学園

Nippon Coll. of Health & P.E. 日本体育大学

Engei H. Sch 園芸高校

Fukazawa 深沢

Yagumo 八雲

Kakinokizaka 柿の木坂

Himonya 碑文谷 En-yū-ji 圓融寺

Meg hor Ma

Hara Nishi-Koi

Futako-Tamagawaen 二子玉川園

Nakamachi 中町

Tama Art Univ. 多摩美術大学

Kaminoge 上野毛

MEGURO DORI (AVE.) 目黒通り

Toritsu-Daigaku 都立大学

Nakane 中根

Taira-machi 平町

Minami Sena

Futako-bashi 二子橋(Br.)

Futako-Shinchi 二子新地

Gotoh Art Mus. 五島美術館

Todoroki 等々力

Tamagawa I.C. 玉川I.C.

Oyamadai 尾山台

Jiyūgaoka 自由が丘

Midorigaoka みどりが丘

Ōokayama 大岡山

Tokyo Inst. of Tech. 東京工業大学

Ōokayama Kita

Noge 野毛

Todoroki Gorge 等々力渓谷

KAN-PACHI DORI (AVE.) 環八通り

Todoroki 等々力

Jōshin-ji 浄真寺 (Kuhonbutsu)

Kuhonbutsu 九品仏

Jiyūgaoka 自由が丘

Okusawa 奥沢

Ishikawa-chō 石川町

Senzoku Park 洗足公園

Shimonoge 下野毛

Tamazutsumi 玉堤

Musashi Inst. of Tech. 武蔵工業大学

Den-en-chōfu 田園調布

Ishikawada

Ishikawa石川台

Yukigaya 雪が谷

Yukigaya-Ōtsuka 雪が谷大塚

Musashi-Shinjō 武蔵新城

Tama Gawa (River) 多摩川

FUCHŌ KAIDO (AVE.) 府中街道

Todoroki Green 等々力緑地

Den-en Chōfu 田園調布

Tamagawaen 多摩川園

Higashi-Tamagawa 東玉川

Se

NAMBU LINE 南武線

KAWASAKI CITY 川崎市

Keihin Kawasaki 京浜川崎センター

Musashi-Shinjō 武蔵新城

Fujitsū General 富士通ゼネラル

Musashi-Nakahara 武蔵中原

Kosugi 小杉

Shin-Maruko 新丸子

Maruko-bashi (Br.) 丸子橋

Den'en Chōfu Honchō 田園調布本町

Numabe 沼部

Den'en Chōfu Hanchō

TŌKAIDŌ-SA 東海道本

Ontakesan OK 御嶽山

Nishi-minemachi 西嶺町

Minami-Kugahara 南久が原

Kugah

Nippon Med. Sch. 日本医大

Musashi-Kosugi 武蔵小杉

Nakahara Ward Office 中原区役所

Den'en Chōfu -Minami 田園調布南

Unoki 鵜の木

Mukaigawara 向河原

NAKAHARA-KU 中原区

Moto-sumiyoshi 元住吉

Shimo-Maruko 下丸子

Musashi-Nitta 武蔵新田

Ch

Chid

Yag

Yaguchino

Kizuki 木月

Naka maruko 中丸子

Mitsubishi Motors 三菱自工

Hirama 平間

Mitsubishi Motors 三菱自工

Kawasaki Tech. H. Sch. 川崎工業高校

Gas-bashi ガス橋(Br.)

Hiyoshi 日吉

Keiō Univ. 慶応大学

Shin-Kawasaki 新川崎

Kashimada 鹿島田

Tōshiba 東芝

Kawasaki Publi G. C. 川崎パブリックコー

Minami-Kase 南加瀬

SAIWAI-K 幸区

Saiwai Ward Office 幸区役所

Ikebukuro 池袋

Ueno 上野

Shinjuku 新宿

Tokyo 東京

Shibuya 渋谷

1 : 70,000

0   1   2 km

23

Rinshino-mori Park
試しの森公園
oyama
高山
Hoshi Coll. of Pharm
星薬科大学
Fudōmae
不動前
Ebara Ramp
荏原ランプ
Togoshi Ramp
戸越ランプ

Kita-Shinagawa
北品川

東京港トンネル
TOKYO-KŌ Tunnel

Ōsaki
大崎

Togoshi-Ginza
戸越銀座

15

Shin-Banba
新馬場

Ōi Thermoelectric Power Plant
大井火力発電所

SHINAGAWA-KU
品川区

Ebara-Nakanobu
荏原中延
niv

Togoshi-Kōen
戸越公園

Shinagawa
Ward Office
品川区役所

Minami-
Shinagawa
南品川

Aomono-
Yokochō
青物横丁

Ōi Ramp
大井ランプ

Hatanoda
旗の台

ŌIMACHI LINE
大井町線

Shimo-Shinmei
下神明

Ōimachi
大井町

Samezu
鮫洲

Ōi Futō(Wharf)
大井ふ頭

Yashio
八潮

Ebaramachi
荏原町

Futaba
二葉

Nishi-Ōi
西大井

Higashi-Ōi
東大井

Minatogaoka Futō Park
みなとが丘ふ頭公園

agahara
中延

Kita-Magome
北馬込

Nishi-Ōi
西大井

Kita-Shinagawa Ramp
北品川ランプ

Tachiaigawa
立会川

WANGAN EXPWY
湾岸道路

niikedai
Naka-
Magome
中馬込

京浜急行線
KEIHIN KYŪKO LINE

Ōikeibajō-mae
大井競馬場前

Ōi-minami Ramp
大井南ランプ

Tōkai
東海

SHINKANSEN
新幹線

Sannō
山王

Minami-Ōi
南大井

Katsushima
勝島

Ōi Racecourse
大井競馬場

Tokyo Freight Terminal Sta.
東京貨物ターミナル駅

Minami-
Magome
南馬込

DAIICHI KEIHIN DŌRO
第一京浜道路

Ōmori
大森

Ōmori-Kaigan
大森海岸

Shin-Heiwa bashi
新平和橋

Heiwajima Ramp
平和島ランプ

Bird Park
(Yachō Kōen)
野鳥公園

aka-
gami

Nishi-Magome
西馬込

Ryushi Mem. Musm
龍子記念館

Ōmori-Kita
大森北

Ryūtsū Center
流通センター

Tokyo Central
Wholesale Market (Ōta)
東京中央卸売市場（大田市場）

Ōta Ward Office
大田区役所

Chūō
中央

Heiwajima
平和島

Ōmorihonchō

Heiwajima
平和島

Keihinjima
京浜島

Ikegami
池上

Honmon-ji
本門寺

ŌTA-KU
大田区

Ōmori-Nishi
大森西

Ōmori-Higashi
大森東

Ōta Tōkō H. Sch.
大田東高校

Ōmori-Higashi H. Sch.
大森東高校

Shōwajima
昭和島

Kegami
池上

Nishi-Kamata
西蒲田

Tōhō Univ.
東邦大学

Ōmorimachi
大森町

Tokyo Rōsai Hosp.
東京労災病院

Higashi-
Yaguchi
矢口

Hasunuma
蓮沼

Umeyashiki
梅屋敷

Kamata
蒲田

Ōmori
-Naka
大森中

Ōmori-Higashi
大森東

Morigasaki Park
森ヶ崎公園

Haneda Undersea Tunnel
羽田海底トンネル

TOKYO INT'L
AIRPORT
東京国際空港
(HANEDA)
(羽田)

amagawa

Shin-Kamata
新蒲田

Kamata
蒲田

Higashi-
Kamata
東蒲田

Ōmori-Minami
大森南

Higashi-
Kōjiya
東糀谷

Kūkō Ramp
空港ランプ

Nishi-Rokugō
西六郷

Naka-Rokugō
中六郷

KEIHIN KYŪKO LINE
京浜急行線

Keikyū-Kamata
京急蒲田

Nishi-Kōjiya
西糀谷

Kōjiya
糀谷

Haneda-seibijō
羽田整備場

agawa-Ōhashi(Br.)
川大橋

KŪKŌ LINE
空港線

DAIICHI KEIHIN DŌRO
第一京浜道路

SANGYŌ DŌRO
産業道路

Ōtorii
大鳥居

Haneda Ramp
羽田ランプ

Zōshiki
雑色

Haginaka
萩中

Anamori-Inari
穴守稲荷

Haneda Kūkō
羽田空港

Haneda
羽田

Haneda-Kūkō
羽田空港

Minami-
Rokugō
南六郷

Honhaneda
本羽田

131

Haneda
羽田

Airport Police Sta.
空港署

Rokugō-dote
六郷土手

Daishi-bashi (Br.)
大師橋

1 : 20,000
0   500m

Ōyama-Higashichō
大山東町

TOBU TŌJŌ LINE
東武東上線

NTT Itabashi
NTT板橋

Ōyaguchi-Kamichō
大谷口上町

Ōyama-Nishichō
大山西町

Ōyamachō
大山町

Ōyama-Kanaichō
大山金井町

ITABASHI-KU
板橋区

Saiwaichō
幸町

KAWAGOE-KAIDŌ (AVE.)

Kumanochō
熊野町

Ikebukuro
池袋

(2)

NTT Minami-Itabashi
NTT南板橋

Naka-maruchō
中丸町

Kumano Jinja
熊野神社

(2)

Toshima
Tokyo Kōts
東京交

Senkawachō
千川町

(2)

Hōnan H. Sch.
豊南高校
(3)

Minamichō
南町

Kita-Ikebukuro Ramp
北池袋ランプ

Shōw
昭

(4)

(1)

Takamatsu
高松
(2)

Hata Sports Plaza
ハタスポーツプラザ

TOSHIMA-KU
豊島区

Takamatsu Ramp
高松ランプ

Kanamechō
要町
(2)

(1)

Ikebukuro
池袋

(2)
92

(1)

(3)

Jōsai Gakuin (Sch)
城西学院

(5)

(1)

Marui
丸井

Tōbu Dept Store
東武デパート

Nishi-Ikebukuro
西池袋

Rikkyō Univ
立教大学

Toshima Tax Office
豊島税務署

Tokyo Met.
Art Space
東京芸術劇場

(1)

Toshima Catholic Ch.
カトリック豊島教会

(4)

(3)

Ikebukuro Police Sta.
池袋警察署

Ike

(1)

Labor Welfare Hall
勤労福祉会館

Hotel
Metropolitan
ホテルメトロポリタン

(H)

Shiinamachi
椎名町

Tōbu Store
東武ストア

SEIBU IKEBUKURO LINE
西武池袋線

Jiyū Gakuen
自由学園
(2)

(1)

32

NAKASENDO (AVE)
中山道

KITA-KU
北区

ashi P.O.
板橋局

Shin-Itabashi
新板橋

Tokyo Gas
東京ガス

Takinogawa
滝野川

Ōji Tech. H. Sch.
王子工業高校

Itabashi
板橋

(1)

(5)

(1)

TOEI MITA LINE

Shimo-
Itabashi
下板橋

SAIKYO LINE

Itabashi-bashi
板橋

Kyū-Nakasendō
旧中山道

(6)

Nishi-Sugamo
西巣鴨

TODEN ARAKAWA LINE

Nishigahara-yonchōme
西ヶ原四丁目

Shin-
Kōshinzuka
新庚申塚

nchō
町

(4)

(7)

(4)

Taishō Univ.
大正大学

(4)

Sch.
Kita-Ikebukuro
北池袋

(4)

Shukutoku Sugamo H. Sch.
淑徳巣鴨高校

Kōshinzuka
庚申塚

(4)

H. Sch.

(1)

(3)

Kami-Ikebukuro
上池袋

Nishi-Sugamo
西巣鴨

(1)

(2)

Sugamo
巣鴨

NTT Sugamo
NTT巣鴨

28

Toshima Chūō Hosp.
豊島中央病院

(2)

MEIJI-DŌRI (AVE)

(1)

Cancer Institute Hosp.
癌研究会病院 (Ganken)

Shinkōshinzukagawa
新庚申塚川

(4)

Sugamo Gakuen (Sch.)
巣鴨学園

Bunkyō H. Sch.
文京高校

Horinouchi-bashi
堀之内橋

(3)

Sugamo-Shinden
巣鴨新田

Kita-Ōtsuka
北大塚

kebukuro
Skating Center

(1)

Jūmonji Gakuen
十文字学園

Toshima
Ward Office
豊島区役所

(2)

Higashi-Ikebukuro
東池袋

Ōtsuka
大塚

Sugamo Police
巣鴨署

ima Public Hall
豊島公会堂

Ōtsuka-Ekimae
大塚駅前

oshi
Mitsukoshi

SUNSHINE CITY
サンシャインシティ

Tenso Jinja
天祖神社

Store

(1)

(3)

H

Sunshine 60 Bldg.
サンシャイン60

Culture Center
文化会館

Mukaihara
向原

(3)

Minami-Ōtsuka
南大塚

Kinka-dō
キンカ堂

93

(4)

KASUGA-DŌRI (AVE)

MARUNOUCHI LINE

Minami-
kebukuro Park
南池袋公園

Higashi-Ikebukuro

(2)

(5)

(2)

33

KITA-KU 北区

Asukayama Park 飛鳥山公園

Takinogawa 滝野川

Ōji Tech. H. Sch. 王子工業高校 ×

Sakuragaoka Girls' H.Sch. 桜丘女子高校 ×

(1)

Takinogawa Kami-Nakazato 滝野川上中里

Takinogawa Police Sta. 滝野川署 ⊗

Takinogawa itchōme 滝野川一丁目

Printing Bureau, Ministry of Financ 大蔵省印刷局

Nishigahara 西ヶ原一丁目地下鉄

(3)

Nishigahara 西ヶ原

Nishigahara yonchōme 西ヶ原四丁目

(4)

Tokyo Univ. of Foreign Studies 東京外国語大学 ×

Kyū Furukawa G. (Former Furukawa G

Taishō Univ. 大正大学 ×

(3)

Shin-Kōshinzuka 新庚申塚

Musashino H. Sch. 武蔵野高校 ×

(7)

Shukutoku Sugamo H.Sch. 淑徳巣鴨高校 ×

(2)

Kagawa Nutrition Jr.Co 女子栄養短大 ×

(6)

Nishi-Sugamo 西巣鴨

Kōshinzuka 庚申塚

(4)

Somei Cemetery (Somei Reien) 染井霊園

(3)

Tokyo Swimming Center 東京スイミングセンター ⊗

NTT Sugamo NTT巣鴨

(4)

Sugamo 巣鴨

(5)

Wholesale Market 卸売市場 ●

Komagome 駒込

Bunkyō H. Sch. 文京高校 ×

Otsuka Deaf Sch. 都立大塚ろう学校 ×

Hongō Gakuen (Sch.) 本郷学園 ×

(4)

Mitsubishi Gym 三菱体育館 ●

(3)

Tōgenuki Jizō 卍 (Kōgan-ji) とげぬき地蔵 (高岩寺)

Kita-Ōtsuka 北大塚

(3)

Shinshō-ji 卍 眞性寺

Seiyu 西友

(2)

Sugamo Shinden 巣鴨新田

Sugamo 巣鴨

(1)

Jūmonji Gakuen (Sch.) 十文字学園 ×

Bunkyō Gakuen (Sc 文京学園

(6)

Ōtsuka 大塚

Ōtsuka-Ekimae 大塚駅前

Sugamo Police Sta. 巣鴨署

Hon-Koma 本駒込

YAMANOTE LINE 山手線

Tenso Jinja 天祖神社 ⊞

Mukaihara 向原 (3)

(1)

Minami-Ōtsuka 南大塚

Tōyō Girls' H.Sch. 東洋女子学園 ×

Koishikawa H 小

(4)

(2)

Sengoku 千石

(3)

NTT Ōtsuka NTT大塚 ©

KASUGA DŌRI (AVE.)

HONGŌ DŌRI (AVE.)

TODEN ARAKAWA LINE 都電荒川線

TOEI MITA LINE 都営三田線

HAKUSAN DŌRI (AVE.)

27

34

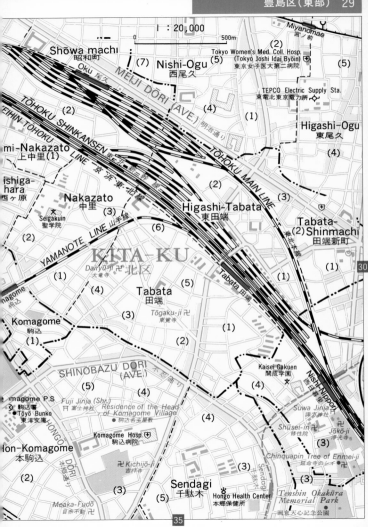

1：20,000

0   500m

Miyanomae
宮ノ前

Shōwa machi
昭和町

Oku 尾久

(7) Nishi-Ogu
西尾久

Tokyo Women's Med. Coll. Hosp.
(Tokyo Joshi Idai Byōin)
東京女子医大第二病院 (5)

MEIJI DORI (AVE.)

明治通り

TEPCO Electric Supply Sta.
東電北東京電力所

(5)

TŌHOKU SHINKANSEN

(2)

(4)

(1)

Higashi-Ogu
東尾久

KEIHIN-TŌHOKU LINE

mi-Nakazato
上中里(1)

TŌHOKU MAIN LINE

(2)

(4)

ishiga-
hara
桓ヶ原

Nakazato
中里

(3)

Higashi-Tabata
東田端

(2)

(3)

Tabata-
Shinmachi
田端新町

Seigakuin
聖学院

(2)

YAMANOTE LINE 山手線

(6)

KITA-KU
北区

(1)

Dairyū-ji 卍
大竜寺

(4)

Tabata
田端

(5)

Tabata 田端

(1)

Komagome
駒込

(1)

Tōgaku-ji 卍
東岳寺

(2)

(1)

magome
駒込

SHINOBAZU DORI
(AVE.) 不忍通り

(5)

(4)

Kaisei Gakuen
開成学園

NISHI-Nippori 西日暮里

Komagome P.S
駒込P.S

Fuji Jinja (Shr.)
富士神社

Residence of the Head
of Komagome Village
駒込名主屋敷

(4)

Suwa Jinja
諏訪神社

Tōyō Bunko
東洋文庫

Shūsei-in
修声院

Jōkō-ji 卍
浄光寺

Komagome Hosp. 卍
駒込病院

lon-Komagome
本駒込

Chinquapin Tree of Enmei-ji
延命寺のシイ

(2)

(3)

Kichijō-ji 卍
吉祥寺

(3)

Sendagi

(3)

Meaka-Fudō 卍
目赤不動

(3)

Sendagi
千駄木

Hongo Health Center
本郷保健所

(5)

Tenshin Okakura
Memorial Park
岡倉天心記念公園

30

Ogu Fire Sta.
尾久消防署

Miyanomae
宮ノ前

Kumanomae
熊ノ前

Tokyo Met. C. of Med. Scl.
都立医療技術短大

Kitatoshima Gakuen
北豊島学園

Road Use
Proficiency Park
交通公園

TODEN ARAKAWA LINE

Women's Med. Coll. Hosp.
(Tokyo Joshi Idai Byōin)
東京女子医大第二病院

(2)

(5)

Higashiogu-sanchome
新電荒川線

(6)

Daigo-Haketa E.
第五峡田小

(4)

TEPCO Electric Supply Sta.
東電北東京電力所

(1)

Higashi-Ogu
東尾久

(4)

Daikyū Jr. H. Sch.
第九中

(2)

Machiya-nichome
町屋二丁目

(6)

Machiya
町屋

(2)

Tabata Chūō Hosp.
田端中央病院

(3)

ARAKAWA-KU
荒川区

(1)

Arakawa
荒川

Tabata-
Shinmachi
田端新町

(2)

Ogu Transformer Sabsta.
尾久変電所

(5)

Daini-
Haketa E. Sch.
第二峡田小

NTT Tabata-Ogu
NTT田端・尾久

(1)

(4)

Arakawa tax office
荒川税務署

(6)

Shin-Mikawashima
新三河島

Arakawa Ward
荒川区役

Nishi-Nippori
西田暮里

Oinuma Hosp.
老沼病院

Daiichi-Haketa E.Sch.
第一峡田小

(1)

Arakawa
Arakawa F

Mikawashima

JOBAN L

Kaisei Gakuen
開成学園

(4)

Daijū Jr. H. Sch.
第十中

Marushin Felt
丸新フェルト

(2)

(6)

(3)

Higashi-N
東日暮里

Suwa Jinja
諏訪神社

Shūsei-in
修性院

Jōkō-Ji
浄光寺

(3)

Daihachi Jr. H. Sch.
第八中

Chinquapin Tree of Enmei-ji
延命寺のカヤ

(3)

Daini-Nippori E. Sch.
第二日暮里小

(5)

Tenshin Okakura
Memorial Park
岡倉天心記念公園

Asakura
Choso Musm
朝倉彫塑館

Nippori

Hotel Lungwood
ホテルラングウッド

(4)

Sendagi
千駄木

Arakawa Maternity Hosp.
荒川産院

Senju-Nakaichō
千住中居町

Senju
千住

Senju-Miyamotochō
千住宮元町

Adachi Ward Office
足立区役所

Kita-Senju

CHIYODA LINE 千代田線

Senju-Midorichō
千住緑町

Senju-Nakachō
千住仲町

rakawa Daigo Jr. H. Sch.
荒川第五中

Senju-Kawarachō
千住河原町

Arakawa Natural Park
荒川自然公園

Senju-Ōhashi
千住大橋

Nippi
ニッピ

Senju-Hashidochō
千住橋戸町

Sewage Disposal Plant
下水処理場

Acrocity
アクロシティ

Wholesale Market
卸売市場

Senju-Ōhashi (Br.)
千住大橋

Arakawa-nanachōme

Minami-Senju Filtration Plant
南千住浄水場

Arakawa Tech. H. Sch.
荒川工業高校

Susanoo Jinja
素盞雄神社

Arakawa-nichōme

Minami-Senju
南千住

南千住野球場
Minami-Senju Baseball Field

Arakawa Sports Center
荒川総合スポーツセンター

Minami-Senju Police Sta.
南千住署

Sumidagawa Freight Sta.
隅田川貨物駅

a Fire Sta.
荒川消防署

kuyakusho
荒川区役所

Minami-Senju

Sun Pearl Arakawa
サンパール荒川

Entsū-ji
円通寺

Minowabashi
三輪橋

Itō-Yōkado Store
イトーヨーカ堂

Ekō-in
回向院

Minowa Hosp.
三ノ輪病院

MEIJI DORI (AVE.)
明治通り

Minowa
三ノ輪

NTT Shirahige
NTT白鬚

Minowa
三ノ輪

Nihonzutsumi
日本堤

1 : 20,000

0   500m

Ryūsen
竜泉

26 Nishi-Ikebukuro 西池袋

(2) Toshima Catholic Ch. ✝
カトリック豊島教会
Nagasaki (1)
長崎
(4)

(3) Ikebukuro Police Sta.
池袋署
Labor Welfare Hall
勤労福祉会館
Hotel
Metropolitan
ホテルメトロポリタン
Jiyū Gakuen
自由学園
(2)

Shiinamachi
椎名町
SEIBU IKEBUKURO LINE

Minami-
Nagasaki Tōbu Store
東武ストア
南長崎 (1)
(5)
(4)

Min
(1)

Mejiro
目白
Mejiro Garden
目白庭園
(3)

(2)

Kawamura-Gakuen
川村学園
(3)

Seibo Jr. Coll. of Nursing
聖母女子短大 ✗
MEJIRO DORI (AVE.)

Holy Mother Hosp.
(Seibo Byōin)
聖母病院
(2)
(4)

Shimo-Ochiai
下落合

Mejirogaoka Ch.
目白ヶ丘教会 ✝

Gakushuin Univ.
学習院大学
(1)

SHINJUKU-KU
新宿区

Otomeyama Park
おとめ山公園

日本造船技術センター
Shipbuilding Research Center
of Japan
Takeda Chemical
武田薬品
Takada
高田

SEIBU SHINJUKU LINE
西武新宿線 (1)

(3)

Kanda Gawa
神田川

(3)

Ochiai Central
Park
落合中央公園

TOZAI LINE 東西線

(3)

Takadanobaba

Big Box Bldg.
ビッグボックス
(2)

WASEDA DORI (AVE.)

Braille Library
日本点字図書館
(1)

Yamate

Otaki-bashi
小滝橋

Plaza Citizen
プラザシチズン (4)

Takadano-baba
高田馬場

Suwa Jinja
諏訪神社

Toyama Danchi (Apts)
都営戸山団地 (4)

Shinjuku Fire Sta.
新宿消防署

Metropolitan Research Lab
of Public Health
都立衛生研究所

Wholesale Market
卸売市場

Nishitoyama Tower Homes
Social Insurance

Toyama Park
戸山公園

Shinjuku-kita P.O.
新宿北局

Shinjuku Sports Center
新宿スポーツセンター

Hozen H. Sch.
保善高校

YOHAN
洋販

Toyama H. Sch.
戸山高

Rehabilita
and Ment
心身障害

(3) Waseda Univ. (Sci. & Engn.)
早稲田大(理工)

38

1 : 20,000

0 500m

Mukaihara
向原

KASUGA DORI AVE.
春日通り

MARUNOUCHI LINE
丸ノ内線

Shin-Ōtsuka
新大塚

Sunshine 60 Bldg.
サンシャイン60

Culture Center
文化会館
(4)

Higashi-Ikebukuro
東池袋

(5)

Higashi-Ikebukuro-
Yonchōme
東池袋四丁目
(6)

(2)

Ōtsuka Hosp.
大塚病院

Minami-
ikebukuro Park
南池袋公園
(2)

ebukuro
袋

(2)

Tōhō Music Sch.
東邦音楽

Tokyo Music Coll.
音楽大学
jin-dō
堂
(3)

Zōshigaya
雑司ヶ谷

Toshimagaoka Ch.
豊島岡教会

Zōshigaya
Cemetery
(Zōshigaya Reien)
雑司が谷霊園

Toshimagaoka Mausoleum
豊島岡御陵

(4)

卍 Gokoku-ji
護国寺

(5)

LINE
線

Kishimojin-
mae
鬼子母神前

(1)

Nichidai Buzan H. Sch.
日大豊山高校

Ōtsuka
大塚

(2)

Chitose-
bashi (Br.)
千登世橋

Zōshigaya
雑司が谷

Gokokuji Ramp
護国寺ランプ

Gokoku-ji
護国寺

(2)

254

(2)

Ochanomizu Univ.
お茶の水女子大学

Sch. for the Blind
盲学校

Otowa
音羽

(2)

Nanzō-in
南蔵院
卍
(2)

Kōdansha
講談社

Ōtsuka Police Sta.
大塚署

Foreign
Training Inst.
外務省研修所
筑波大付属高校
Tsukuba Univ. H.

34

Univ. of Tokyo
Faculty of Medicine
Branch Hosp.
東大付属病院
分院
(3)

(2)

(1)

Japan Women's Univ.
日本女子大学

Mejirodai
目白台
(1)

St. Mary's Cathedral
東京カテドラル聖マリア大聖堂

Otowa
音羽

Omokagebashi
面影橋

(1)

Shin Edogawa Park
新江戸川公園

Dokkyō Gakuen (Sch.)
独協学園

(3)

(1)

Waseda
早稲田

Kansen'en Park
甘泉園公園 (1)

(1)

Chinzan-sō
椿山荘
(2)

Sekiguchi
関口

Waseda
早稲田
(3)

Ōkuma Hall
大隈会館

Edogawabashi
江戸川橋

Waseda Ramp
早稲田ランプ

ng Inst.
所 ●

Totsuka-
machi
戸塚町

Ōkuma Garden
大隈庭園

Waseda Univ.
早稲田大学

Ana Hachiman
穴八幡

Gakushūin
(Girls' Sch.)
学習院（女子）
for the Physically
Handica-
pped

Waseda H. Sch.
早稲田高校

Baba-
shitacho

Waseda
Tsurumakichō
早稲田鶴巻町

Waseda Jitsugyo
早稲田実業

Akagidai H Sch.
赤城台高校

Yamabukichō
山吹町

Waseda
Univ. Mem. Hall
早稲田大学記念会堂

Wasedamachi 早稲田町

Waseda

Enoki
chō
榎町

Nakazatocho
中里町

39

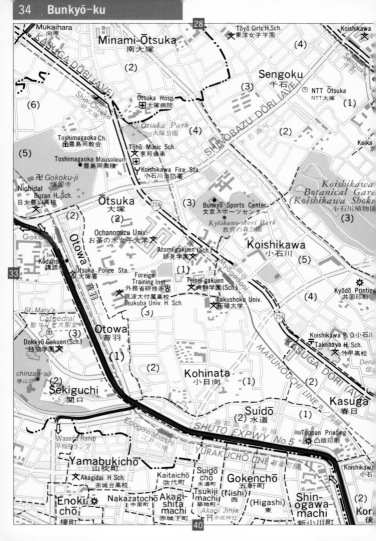

Mukaihara
向原
Minami-Ōtsuka
南大塚
(2)

KASUGA DORI AVE.

Shin-Ōtsuka
新大塚

(6)

(5)

Toshimagaoka Ch.
豊島岡教会
Toshimagaoka Mausoleum
豊島岡御陵

Nichidai
Buzan H. Sch.
日大豊山高校

Gokoku-ji
護国寺

Gokoku-ji
護国寺

Kōdansha
講談社

Ōtsuka Hosp.
大塚病院

Ōtsuka Park
大塚公園
(4)

Tōhō Music Sch.
東邦音楽
Koishikawa Fire Sta.
小石川消防署

Ōtsuka
大塚
(2)

Otowa
音羽

(2)

Ochanomizu Univ.
お茶の水女子大学
(2)

Ōtsuka Police Sta.
大塚署

Foreign
Training Inst.
外務省研修所
Tsukuba Univ. H. Sch.
筑波大付属高校
(3)

St. Mary's
Cathedral
聖マリア大聖堂

Dokkyō Gakuen (Sch.)
独協学園高校
(3)

Otowa
音羽
(1)

chinzan-so
椿山荘
(2)

Sekiguchi
関口

Edogawabashi
江戸川橋

Waseda Ramp
早稲田ランプ

Yamabukichō
山吹町

Akagidai H. Sch.
赤城台高校

Enoki-
chō
榎町

Nakazatochō
中里町

Kaitaichō
改代町

Akagi-
shita-
machi
赤城下町

Suidō-
chō
水道町

Tsukiji-
machi
築地町

Suidō-
chō
水道町
(Nishi)
西
Akagi Jinja
赤城神社

Tōyō Girls'H.Sch.
東洋女子学園
(4)

Koishikawa
小石川

Sengoku
千石
(3)

Sengoku
千石

NTT Ōtsuka
NTT大塚
(1)

Keika
桂華

SHINOBAZU DORI AVE.

(2)

Koishikawa
Botanical Garden
(Koishikawa Shokubutsuen)
小石川植物園

(3)

Bunkyō Sports Center
文京スポーツセンター
Kyōikuno-mori Park
教育の森公園

(3)

Koishikawa
小石川
(5)

Atomi-gakuen (Sch.)
跡見学園

(1)

Teisei-gakuen
貞静学園 (Sch.)
Takushoku Univ.
拓殖大学

(4)

Myōgadani
茗荷谷

Kyōdō Printing
共同印刷

Koishikawa P. O.小石川
Takehaya H. Sch.
竹早高校

Den-
伝

Kohinata
小日向
(1)

MARUNOUCHI LINE

KASUGA DORI AVE.

Kasuga
春日

Suidō
水道
(2)

(1)

SHUTO EXPWY No.5

YURAKUCHO LINE

Toppan Printing
凸版印刷

Gokenchō
五軒町

Koishikawa
小石川

Shin-
ogawa-
machi
新小川町

Kor
後
(2)

28

33

40

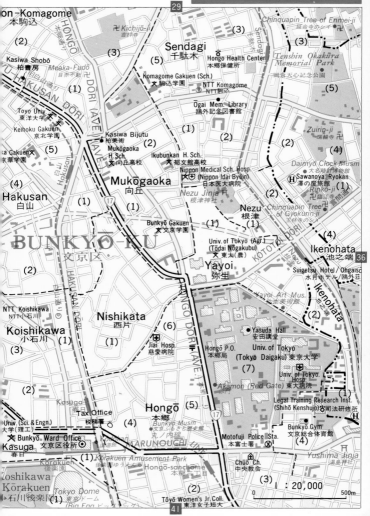

on-Komagome
本駒込
(2)

卍 Kichijō-ji
吉祥寺

Sendagi
千駄木
(5)

Chinquapin Tree of Enmei-ji
延命寺のシイ卍
(3)

Kasiwa Shobō
柏書房
(1)

Meaka-Fudō
目赤不動卍

Hongo Health Center
本郷保健所

Tenshin Okakura
Memorial Park
岡倉天心記念公園

(3)

Komagome Gakuen (Sch.)
文 駒込学園

NTT Komagome
NTT駒込

(5)

Toyo Univ.
東洋大学
(1)

Keihoku Gakuen
京北学園

Ōgai Mem. Library
鴎外記念図書館

Zuirin-ji
瑞輪寺卍
(4)

ka Gakuen文
京華学園
(5)

Kasiwa Bijutu
柏美術
Mukōgaoka
H. Sch.
文 向丘高校
(2)

Ikubunkan H. Sch.
文 郁文館高校
(1)

(2)

Daimyō Clock Musm
大名時計博物館

Sawanoya Ryokan
澤の屋旅館
(H)
(1)

(4)

Hakusan
白山
(1)

Mukōgaoka
向丘
(1)

Nippon Medical Sch. Hosp.
(Nippon Idai Byōin)
日本医大病院

Nezu Jinja 卍
根津神社

Rinpō-ji
卍輪法寺
(2)

Chinquapin Tree
of Gyokurin-ji
玉林寺のシイ卍

BUNKYŌ-KU
文京区

Bunkyō Gakuen
文 文京学園
(1)

Nezu
根津
(1)

(4)

(2)

Univ. of Tokyo (Agr.)
(Tōdai Nōgakubu)
東大(農)

Yayoi
弥生

Ikenohata
池之端

36

NTT Koishikawa
NTT小石川

Nishikata
西片

Suigetsu Hotel / Ohgaisō
水月ホテル / 鴎外荘
(2)

Yayoi Art Mus.
弥生美術館

Ikenohata
池之端

Koishikawa
小石川
(1)

(6)

(2)

(3)

(1)

Jiai Hosp.
慈愛病院

Yasuda Hall
安田講堂

Univ. of Tokyo
(Tokyo Daigaku) 東京大学

Univ. of Tokyo
Hosp. 東大病院

Hongō P.O.
本郷局
(7)

Univ. (Sci. & Engn.)
大学(理工)

Tax Office
税務署

Hongō
本郷
(5)

Akamon (Red Gate) 東大赤門

Legal Training Research Inst.
(Shihō Kenshujo) 司法研修所

文 Bunkyō Ward Office
文京区役所

Kasuga
春日

Bunkyō Musm
文京ふるさと歴史館

Motofuji Police Sta.
本富士署

Bunkyō Gym
文京総合体育館
(4)

(H)

Kōrakuen Amusement Park
ゆうえんち

MARUNOUCHI
丸ノ内

Hongō-sanchōme
本郷三丁目

Chūō Ch.
中央教会

Yushima Jinja
湯島神社

Koshikawa-
Kōrakuen
石川後楽園

Tokyo Dome
東京ドーム
(Big Egg ビッグエッグ)
(1)

Tōyō Women's Jr. Coll.
東洋女子短大
(2)

: 20,000

500m

1 : 20,000
500m

30

Nippori JR
日暮里

Tenshin Okakura
Memorial Park
岡倉天心記念公園

Asakura
Choso Musm
朝倉彫塑館

Daini-Nippori E. Sch
第二日暮里小 (5)

Hotel Lungwood
ホテルラングウッド

(4)

(3)

Takenodai H. Sch
竹台高校

Musm of Calligraphy
書道博物館

Enko-ji
卍円光寺

Negisl
根岸

(4)

Yanaka Cemetery
(Yanaka Reien)
谷中霊園

(5)

(7)

Yanaka
谷中

Jōmei-in
卍浄名院

Zuirin-ji
瑞輪寺 卍

(2)

(4)

(6)

(2)

Ueno-
Sakuragi (Uguisudani)
上野桜木

下谷病院
Shitaya Hosp.

Onoterusaki Jinja
小野照崎神社

Shitaya
下谷

(3)

(2)

Daimyo Clock Musm
大名時計博物館

Kan'ei-ji (1)
卍寛永寺

(2)

Kishimojin
鬼子母神

Triya

Sawanoya Ryokan
澤の屋旅館 H

Rinko-ji (1)
卍臨江寺

Tokugawa Graveyard
徳川家墓地

Tokyo Nat'l Univ. of Fine Arts & Music
(Tokyo Geijutsu Daigaku)東京芸術大学

Nat'l Musm
国立博物館

Ueno P.O.
上野

Ueno-S
H. Sch

Chinquapin Tree
of Gyokurin-ji
玉林寺のシ

Ryokan
Katsutaro Ueno H. Sch
旅館勝太郎 上野高校

Ueno Library
上野図書館

Hakubutsukan・
Dōbutsuen
博物館・動物園

Ueno Park 上野公園

Tokyo Met. Art Musm
東京都美術館

Ryōdaishi
両大師

Kita-Uen
北上野

Ikenohata
池之端

Ueno Zoo
上野動物園 H

Ueno-Kōen
上野公園

76

Ishibashi Mem. Hall
石橋記念ホール

Ikenohata
池之端

Suigetsu Hotel / Ohgaiso
水月ホテル・鴎外荘 H

Nat'l Musm of Western
国立西洋美術館

Oshoga月
東照宮

UENO
上野

(7)

(4)

Tokyo Met. Festival Hall
(Tokyo Bunka Kaikan)
東京文化会館

Aquarium
水族館

Taito Ward Office
台東区役所
◎台東区役所

(6)

Univ. of TOKYO
東京大学

Shinobazuno-ike
不忍池

Japan Art Academy
日本芸術院

(5)

Inaricho 稲荷町

Ueno Park
上野公園

Ueno Ramp
上野ランプ

Higashi-
Ueno
東上野

Moto-

Univ. of Tokyo.
Hosp.
東大病院

Benten-dō
卍弁天堂

下谷神社
Shitaya Jinja

(2)

Legal Training Research Inst.
(Shihō Kenshujo)
司法研修所

Ueno (4)
上野

(1)

Bunkyo Gym
文京総合体育館
(4)

Takara Hotel
タカラホテル H

(2)

(1)

Hakuō
白鴎高
文

Yushima Jinja
湯島神社

(4)

KASUG

Yushima
湯島

(2) 湯島

(3)

(1)

(3)

Okachimachi

(5)

(3)

Kojima
小島

(2)

77

42

31

NTT Shirahige
NTT白髭

Minowa
三ノ輪
(1)

(2)

Nihonzutsumi
日本堤

Kiyokawa
清川

Hashiba
橋場
(1)

(2)

Ryūsen
(2) 竜泉

(3)

Ichiyō Mem. Hall
一葉記念館

(1)

(2)

Toy Museum
(Gangu Shiryōkan)
玩具資料館

hitaya
olice Sta.
谷署⊗

(1)

Senzoku
千束
(4)

⊗ Higashi-
Asakusa
東浅草

(2)

Imado
今戸
(2)

Taitō Hosp.
台東病院⊗

Nihonzutsumi Fire Sta.
日本堤消防署

Iriya
入谷
(2)

Ōtori Jinja
鷲神社

NTT Yoshiwara
NTT吉原
(3)

⊕Seiai Hosp.
聖愛病院
(5)

(1)

(2)

Confectionery Hall
菓子会館
(2)

Taitō Comm. H. Sch.
台東商業高校

TAITŌ-KU
台東区

Asakusa Police Sta.
浅草署⊗
(4)

(1)

KOTOTOI DORI (AVE.)

(3)

Asakusa
浅草

Matsuchiyama Park
待乳山公園

Sakura-bashi
桜橋

校 (4)

78

Nishi-
Asakusa
西浅草
(3)

(2)

Matsuchiyama Shōden 卍
待乳山聖天

(6)

(7)

Kototoi-bashi
言問橋

tsugaya
が谷
(3)

Sumida Park
隅田公園

Senso-ji (temple)
浅草寺

Asakusa
西浅草
(2)

Asakusa Park
浅草公園

Hanakawado
花川戸

(2)

Asakusa Public Hall 浅草
浅草公会堂

Asakusa
浅草

TOBU ISESAKI LINE
東武伊勢崎線

suya
谷
)

Kitchenware
Town
Kappabashi
合羽橋

Asakusa
西浅草
(2)

Tokyo Higashi Hongan-ji
東京東本願寺

(1)

Sumida Ward Office
墨田区役所

LINE
銀座線

DORI AVE.

Asakusa P.O.
浅草郵便局

Kaminarimon
雷門

Azuma-bashi
吾妻橋

ARP Pl./arpla Azumabashi
リバーピア吾妻橋

Azumabashi
吾妻橋
(3)

4)

(2)

NTT

Komagata-bashi(Br.)
駒形橋

(1)

Homo-azumobashi
本所吾妻橋

Tawaramachi
田原町
(2)

(4)

Kotobuki
寿
(1)

Asakusa
浅草

Komagata
駒形

Komagata Ramp
駒形ランプ

Higashi-Komagata
東駒形
(3)

3)

(1)

(3)

Waterbus
水上バス

(1)

(2)

Health Center
保健所

T AVE.)春日通り

Umaya-
bash
厩橋

SUMIDA-KU
墨田区

uji
ル

43

1 : 20,000
500m

Nihonkaku
日本閣

Higashi-Nakano
東中野

CHUO LINE
中央線

Higashi-Nakano
東中野
(1)

(4)

Wholesale Market
卸売市場

Shinjuku Fire Sta.
新宿消防署

Metropolitan Research Lab
of Public Health
都立衛生研究所
Nishitoyama Tower Homes
Social Insurance
Central Hosp
社会保険中央病院

Shinjuku Sports
新宿スポーツ

Hozen H. Sch.
保善高校 (3)

Waseda U

(3)

Hyakunincho
百人町
(2)

Kaijo H. Sch.
海城学園

Oku
大久

YAMANOTE LINE
山手線

OKUBO DORI (AVE.)大久保通り

Kita-Shinjuku
北新宿

Okubo 大久保

Lotte
ロッテ

SHINJ
新宿

Shin-Okubo 新大久保

SEIBU SHINJUKU LINE 西武新宿線

(1)

(1)

NTT Shinjuku
NTT新宿

(2)

Shinjuku Tax Office
新宿税務署

(1)

NTT

(1)

Shinjuku Red C
Maternity Ho
新宿赤十字

ŌME KAIDŌ (AVE.)

Naruko Tenjinsha
鳴子天神社

青梅街道

Health Center
新宿保健所

90

(8)

(7)

88

Kabukicho
歌舞伎町

Seibu Shinjuku 西武新宿

(1)

Shinjuku Ward Office
新宿区役所

(5)

Tokyo Med. Coll. Hosp.
東京医大病院

Nomura Bldg
野村ビル

(6)

Mitsui Bldg
三井ビル

Shinjuku

(3)

紀伊国屋
Kinokuniya

伊勢丹
Isetan

Shi

Tokyo Hilton Int'l
東京ヒルトンインターナショナル

Dai-Ichi Seimei Bldg
第一生命ビル

Sumitomo Bldg
住友ビル

池田山ハルク
Odakyu Halc

Odakyu Dept Store
小田急デパート

(1)

Mitsukoshi
三越

MY CITY
マイシティー

三越

Marui
丸井

Hotel Century Hyatt
ホテルセンチュリーハイアット

Kōgakuin Univ.
工学院大学

Keio Plaza Hotel
京王プラザホテル

Shinjuku P.O.
新宿局

Keio Dept Store
京王デパート

Shinjuku
新宿

MARU

Kumano Jinja

Shinjuku
Central Park
新宿中央公園

(4)

Nishi-Shinjuku
西新宿

Tokyo Met. Gov't
東京都庁

NS Bldg
NSビル
(2)

(20)

KDD Bldg
KDDビル

(4)

Tenryu
Tenryu

Shinjuku
新宿

Kantō Gakuen
(Sch.)
関東学園

Shinjuku Ramp
新宿ランプ

Washington Hotel
ワシントンホテル

91

JR東京総合病院
JR Tokyo General Hosp

89

Tokyo Gas
東京ガス

(3)

Bunka Women's Coll.
文化女子大学
Bunka Gakuen
Costume Mus.
文化学園服飾博物館

(2)

ODAKYU LINE 小田急線

新宿パークホテル
Shinjuku Park Hotel

YOYOGI
代々木

32

44

Waseda-Tsurumakichō
早稲田鶴巻町

Toyama H. Sch.
戸山高校

Gakushūin (Girls' Sch.)
学習院（女子）

Waseda H. Sch.
早稲田高校

Waseda Jitsugyo
早稲田実業

(3)

Rehabilitation Center for the Physically
and Mentally Handicapped
心身障害者福祉センター

Ana Hachiman
穴八幡

Baba-
Shitachō

Wasedamachi 早稲田町

Waseda
Univ. Mem. Hall
早稲田大学大隈記念講堂

Parking Bldg.
駐車場

Toyama
戸山

Waseda Univ.
早稲田大学

(1)

Waseda-
minamichō
早稲田南町

Sōsan-ji

(2)

Toyama Heights Apts
戸山ハイツ

Nat'l Hosp.
Med. Service Center
(Iryō Center)
国立病院医療センター

Kikuichō
喜久井町

Bentenchō
弁天町

Jōrin-ji
常林寺

OKUBO DORI AVE.
大久保通り

Statistics Bureau
統計局

Haramachi
原町

U-KU

Wakamatsuchō
若松町

Aikidō World H.Q.
(Honbu Dōjō)
合気道本部道場

(7)

Nukebenten
抜弁天

Tokyo Women's
Med. Coll.
東京女子医大

Seijō H. Sch.
成城高校

Ichigaya-
Yanagichō
市谷柳町

Ichigaya-
Kōrachō
市谷甲良町

NTV Golf Garden
日本テレビゴルフガーデン

Yochōmachi
余丁町

Ichigaya-
Yakuōjimachi
市谷薬王寺町

(6)

Nishimuki Tenjin
西向天神

Kawadachō
河田町

Korean School
韓国学校

juku Culture Center
新宿文化センター

Fuji Television
フジテレビ

Ichigaya-
Nakanochō
市谷仲之町

Tokyo Med. Coll.
東京医科大学

Sumiyoshi-
chō

Ichigaya-
Honmurachō
市谷本村町

Jinja

(5)

Koishikawa Tech.
H. Sch.
小石川工業高校

Ichigaya-Daimachi
市谷台町

Katamachi
片町

Tomihisachō
富久町

Kōsei Nenkin Hall
厚生年金会館

Seijo Gakuen (Sch.)
成女学園

Akebonobashi
曙橋

YASUKUNI DORI AVE.
靖国通り

TOEI SHINJUKU LINE

NTT Yotsuya
NTT四谷

都営新宿線

Sakamachi
坂町

(2)

Taisoji

(1)

Aizumi-
chō
愛住町

Funa-
machi
舟町

Arakichō
荒木町

San'eichō
三栄町

SHINJUKU DORI (AVE.)
新宿通り

Yotsuya
四谷

(3)

Yotsuya Fire Sta.
四谷消防署

Shinjuku-gyoenmae
新宿御苑前

Yotsuya-sanchōme
四谷三丁目

Yotsuya 四谷

njuku Gyoen
u Imperial Gardens
新宿御苑

Naitōchō
内藤町

Daikyōchō
大京町

Samonchō

Yotsuya Police Sta.
四谷署

(2)

Bunka Broadcasting
(Bunka Hōsō)
文化放送

(2)

(1)

Noguchi Mem. Hall
記念館

Sugachō
須賀町

33

40

45

Yamabukicho
山吹町

34

Kaitaichō
改代町

Suido
chō
水道町

Gokenchō
五軒町

Koishikaw
小石

Akagidai H Sch.
赤城高校

Tsukiji
machi
築地町

Akagi-
shita
machi
赤城下町

Akagi (Nishi)
西

(Higashi)
東

Shino-
gawa-
machi
新小川町

(2)

K

Nakazatochō
中里町

Enoki-
chō
榎町

Higashi-
Enokichō

Tenjinchō
天神町

Akagi Jinja
赤城神社

Akagi
Tsukudo-Hachiman
-motomachi
筑土八幡町

Kosei-nenkin Hosp
厚生年金病院

Shimomi-
yabichō
下宮比町

Shiroganechō
白銀町

SHINJUKU-KU
新宿区

Bentenchō
弁天町

Jōrin-ji
淨輪寺

Kagurazaka
神楽坂

Tsukudo-
Hachiman

Tsukudo-
chō
津久戸町

Agebachō
揚場町

Minami-
Enokichō
南榎町

Yaraichō
矢来町

Yokoteramachi
横寺町

Iwatochō
岩戸町

Bishamonten
毘沙門天（善国寺）

Kagurazaka
神楽坂

Jidabashi
飯田橋

Kagura
Police Ho
(Keisatsu B
警察署

Obunsha Publ
旺文社

Tansumachi
簞笥町

Fukuromachi
袋町

Central Plaza
セントラルプラザ

Wakamiyachō
若宮町

Science Univ.
Tokyo
東京理科大学

Ichigaya Comm. H Sch.
市谷商業高校

Kitamachi
北町

Nippon Dental
日本歯科大学

Yamabushi Ushigome P.O.
牛込局

Ichigaya-
Tanagidaichō
市谷柳町

Ichigaya-
Kōrachō
市谷加賀町

Nijukkimachi
二十騎町

Nandō-
machi
納戸町

Nakachō
中町

Minamichō
南町

Ichigaya
Funagawara
machi
市谷船河原町

Teishin Hosp
逓信病院

(2)

Ichigaya-
Yakuojimachi
市谷薬王寺町

Ichigaya-Kagachō
市谷加賀町

(2)

(1)

Ichigaya
Harai-katamachi
払方町

Ichigaya
Sadoharachō
市谷左内坂町

Kaetsu Girls' H Sch.
嘉悦女子高校

Shirayuri Gak
白百合学園

Dai Nippon Printing
大日本印刷

Ichigaya
Takajōmachi
市谷鷹匠町

Hōsei Univ.
法政大学

Memorial Musm
of the Printing Bureau
大蔵省印刷局記念館

Ichigaya
Sanaichō
市谷砂土原町

Ichigaya
Chōenjimachi
市谷長延寺町

Miwata Gakuen (Sch.)
三輪田学園

Yasukuni Jinja
靖国神社

Ichigaya-Honmurachō
市谷本村町

Ichigaya Hachiman
市谷八幡

Kudan-Kita
九段北

Ground-Self Defense Force Ichigaya Post
陸上自衛隊市ヶ谷駐屯地

Ichigaya-Hachimanchō
市谷八幡町

Kōjimachi P.O.
麹町局

Kudan-Minami
九段南

Nisho-
西

Grand Hill Ichigaya
グランドヒル市ヶ谷

Ichigaya-Tamachi
市ヶ谷田町

Tokyo Kasei Gakuin
東京家政学院

Otsuma Women
大妻女子大

YASUKUNI DORI (AVE.)
靖国通

Ichigaya
市ヶ谷

Sakamachi
坂町

Salvation Army
救世軍

Ichigaya
市ヶ谷

Yonbanchō
四番町

YWCA

Emb. of Vatican
ローマ法王庁大使館

Sanbanchō
三番町

Chide
Milita

San'eichō
三栄町

Shinjuku Historical Musm
新宿歴史博物館

Gobanchō
五番町

Tokyo Chinese School
東京中華学校
Chinese School

Chiyoda Jogakkan (Sch.)
千代田女学園

Honshiochō
本塩町

Yoshi Gakuin
女子学院

Yotsuya Tax Office
四谷税務署

Rokubanchō
六番町

Ichibanchō
一番町

Yotsuya
四谷

Futaba-gakuen (Sch.)
雙葉学園

NTV
日本テレビ

Emb of Luxembourg
ルクセンブルク大使館

Diamond Hotel
ダイヤモンド

Bunka Broadcasting
(Bunka Hōsō)
文化放送

Nibanchō
二番町

Emb of Israel
イスラエル大使館

Hanzōmon
半蔵門

1:20,000

500m

Emb. of Belgium
ベルギー大使館

Kōjimachi
麹町

(6)

(5)

(4)

(3)

20

(2)

(1)

46

MARUNOUCHI

● Bunkyo Ward Office 文京区役所 ◎
Kasuga
春日
Kōrakuen Amusement Park
後楽園ゆうえんち
Hongō-sanchōme
本郷三丁目
Chūō Ch. 中央教会
Yushima Jinj 湯島神社
文京区
BUNKYO-KU
(3)
Yushima
湯島
(3)

Koishikawa-Kōrakuen
小石川後楽園
Tokyo Dome
東京ドーム
(Big Egg) ビッグエッグ
(1)
Tōyō Women's Jr. Coll.
東洋女子短大
Nippon Shinpan
日本信販
(2)

Kōraku
後楽
● Kōraku Hall 後楽園ホール
● Yellow Bldg 黄色いビル
(1)
Noh Theater
能楽堂
Kyūsuisho Park
給水所公苑
Juntendo Univ
順天堂大学
Hitachi Hosp.
日立病院

● Polyteck H. Sch.
工芸高校
Oln
Showa 昭和
Kanda Myōjin
神田明神
(1)

水道橋
Suidōbashi
CHŪŌ LINE 中央線
Tokyo Med. & Dent. Univ.
東京医科歯科大学
Yushima-Seid
湯島聖堂

dabashi
飯田橋
Misakichō
(3) 三崎町
Saru-
gakuchō
Ochanomizu
御茶ノ水
(2)
75

Nihon Univ.
日本大学 (法)
猿楽町
Surugadai
駿河台
Nikorai-dō
ニコライ堂

Nishi-Kanda
西神田
(3)
Nishi-Kanda Ramp
西神田ランプ
Meiji Univ.
明治大学
Nihon Univ.
日本大学
(3)
Awajichō
淡路町
(2)

Jinbōchō
神保町
Senshu Univ.
専修大学
Kudan P.O.
九段局
Jinbocho
神保町
YASUKUNI
Ogawamachi
小川町(2)
42

ch. el Grand Palace
ルグランドパレス
Kudan Minami
九段南
Hitotsu-
bashi
一ツ橋
Chiyoda Ward Office
千代田区役所
Kyōritsu Gakuen
共立学園
Nishiki-chō
錦町
Kanda Police Sta
神田署
Tsukasa
machi
司町

Nippon Budōkan
日本武道館
Kitanomaru Park
北の丸公園
Shimizu-mon
清水門
Tax Office
税務署
Hitotsubashi Ramp
一ツ橋ランプ
Uchikanda
内神田

Kitanomaru-kōen
北の丸公園
Science Mus.
科学技術館
Tokyo Nat'l Mus. of Modern Art
東京国立近代美術館
NTT
Mainichi
毎日
Meteorological Agency
気象庁
Kandabashi Ramp
神田橋ランプ

Daikanchō Ramp
代官町ランプ
Kitanomaru Ramp
北の丸ランプ
Takebashi
竹橋
East Imperial Garden
(Kōkyo Higashi Gyoen)
皇居東御苑
Yomiuri
読売
Sankei
サンケイ

CHIYODA-KU
千代田区
Chiyoda
千代田
Ōtemon
大手門
Otemachi
大手町
(2)

Imperial Household Agency
(Kunaichō) 宮内庁
Imperial Guard H.Q.
皇宮警察本部
Ōtemon
大手門
Palace Hotel
パレスホテル
JTB

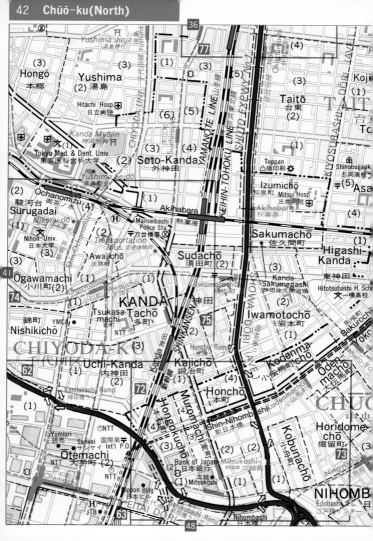

(3) Hongō 本郷

Yushima Jinja 湯島神社

(3) Yushima (2) 湯島

Hitachi Hosp. 日立病院

Kanda Myōjin 神田明神

Tokyo Med. & Dent. Univ. 東京医科歯科大学

Yushima Seidō 湯島聖堂

(2) Soto-Kanda 外神田

(2) Ochanomizu 御茶ノ水

Surugadai 駿河台

Nikolai-dō ニコライ堂

Nihon Univ. 日本大学

(3) Ogawamachi 小川町(2)

Transportation Mus. 交通博物館

Manseibashi Police Sta. 万世橋署

Awajichō 淡路町

(1) Akihabara 秋葉原

Sudachō 須田町(2)

KANDA Tachō 神田 多町

Tsukasa-machi 司町

Nishikichō 錦町

YMCA

NTT

Uchi-Kanda 内神田

CHIYODA-KU 千代田区

Kandabashi Ramp 神田橋ランプ

Yomiuri 読売

Sankei サンケイ

Int'l P.O. 国際局

Ōtemachi 大手町(2)

NTT

NTT

Nippon Bldg 日本ビル

JTB

Otemachi

Taitō 台東(2)

TAITŌ

Koji

Shinobugaoka 忍岡高校

Izumichō 和泉町

Mitsui Hosp. 三井病院

Toppan 凸版印刷

Asa

Sakumachō 佐久間町

Higashi Kanda 東神田

Hitotsubashi H. Sch. 一橋高校

Kanda Sakumagashi 神田佐久間河岸

Iwamotochō 岩本町

SHINKANSEN

SHŌWA DŌRI

Honcho Ramp 本町ランプ

Kajichō 鍛冶町(1)

Honchō 本町

Muromachi 室町

Hongokuchō 本石町

Shin-Nihombashi 新日本橋

Bank of Japan 日本銀行

Mitsukoshi-mae 三越前

Mitsukoshi 三越

Kodenma-chō 小伝馬町

Kobunachō 小舟町

Oden- ma- chō 大伝馬町

Bakuroch

Horidome- chō 堀留町

CHŪŌ 中央

NIHOMB

Edobashi I.C. 江戸橋

Ningyōch

Edobashi Ramp 江戸橋ランプ

Nihombashi 日本橋

EITAI DŌRI

KU

(1)　Kotobuki
　　　寿　(3)

Misuji
三筋　　(1)

DORI (AVE.)　(4)

Kuramae
蔵前(3)

Tax Office
税務署

Kuramae-bashi
蔵前橋

(2)

(3)

Kuramae Police Sta.
蔵前署

Kuramae Tech.
H. Sch.
蔵前工業高

Ryōgoku Public Hall
両国公会

(2)

Yanagibashi
柳橋

(1)

Komagata　37

Umaya-bashi
厩橋

(Br.)

Lion
ライオン　(1)

Yokoami
横網

Dōai Mem. Hosp.
同愛　病院

Reconstruction Mem. Hall
東京都慰霊堂

Yasuda Gakuen (Sch.)
安田学園(高)

Yasuda Garden
旧安田庭園

Sumō Stadium
(Kokugikan)
国技館

Nichidai Daiichi H. Sch.
日大一高

(1)

Health Center
保健所

(2)　Honjo　(3)
　　　本所

SUMIDA-KU
墨田区

(1)

KURAMAEBASHI DŌRI
(AVE.)

Ishiwara
石原

Kamezawa
亀沢

(1)

SŌBU LINE　総武線

Ryōgoku P.O.
両国局

(H)

(H)　Ryōgoku
　　　両国

KEIYŌ　DŌRO (AVE.)

(14)

Ryōgoku-bashi (Br.)
両国橋

Ryōgoku
両国

(2)

Eko-in 卍
回向院

(2)

Higashi-
Nihombashi
東日本橋

NTT Hamachō
NTT浜町
(1)

Tokyo TV
東京
テレビセンター

Ryōgoku I.C.
両国インター

(3)

Hamachō
浜町

Ryōgoku
両国

(2)

Honjo Police Sta.
本所署

(1)

Midori
緑

SHUTO EXPWY No.7

Chitose
(2)　千歳　(3)

Shin-Ohashi
新大橋

(2)

Tatekawa
立川
(1)

NTT本所
NTT Honjo

Kikukawa
菊川

TOEI SHINJUKU LINE　都営新宿線

samatsuchō
Meiji-za
明治座

izawachō

gyōchō
形町

Hamachō
浜町
(3)

Hamachō Ram

Suitengū (Str.)
水天宮

Shin-
Ohashi
新大橋

(Br.)

Bashō Mem. Hall

(1)　Tokiwa　(2)
　　　常盤

(3)　Morishita
　　　森下(4)

Takabashi
高橋

江東区
KOTO-KU

1 : 20,000

0　　　　　　500m

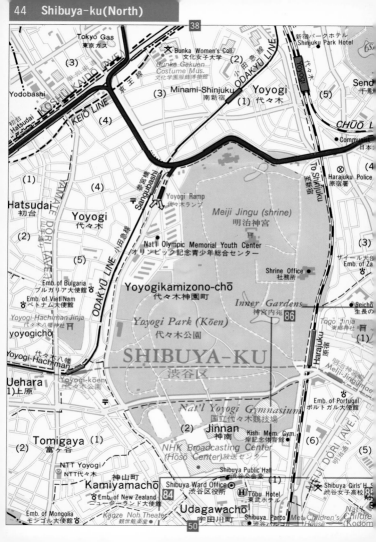

38

Tokyo Gas
東京ガス

(3)

新宿パークホテル
Shinjuku Park Hotel

ODAKYU LINE

Send
千馬

(5)

KOSHU KAIDO AVE.

Bunka Women's Coll.
文化女子大学
Bunka Gakuen
Costume Mus.
文化学園服飾博物館

(2)

(3) Minami-Shinjuku
南新宿

Yoyogi
代々木
(1)

CHŪO L

Yodobashi

初台
Hatsudai

KEIO LINE

(4)

(3)

Communi
日本

Harajuku
Police
原宿署

(4)

(1)

Hatsudai
初台

(4)

参宮橋
Sangubashi

Yoyogi Ramp
代々木ランプ

Meiji Jingu (shrine)
明治神宮

ザイール大使
Emb. of Za

(3)

Yoyogi
代々木

(2)

Nat'l Olympic Memorial Youth Center
オリンピック記念青少年総合センター

(5)

Emb. of Bulgaria
ブルガリア大使館
Emb. of Viet Nam
ベトナム大使館

Yoyogikamizono-chō
代々木神園町

Shrine Office
社務所

Inner Gardens
神宮内苑

86

Seichō
生長の

Yoyogi-Hachiman Jinja
代々木八幡神社
yoyogichō

Yoyogi Park (Kōen)
代々木公園

Togo Jinja
東郷神社

(1)

Yoyogi-Hachiman

SHIBUYA-KU
渋谷区

Harajuku

明治神宮前
Meiji-Jingūmae

Yoyogi-kōen
代々木公園

Uehara
上原

(1)

Emb. of Portugal
ポルトガル大使館

Nat'l Yoyogi Gymnasium
国立代々木競技場

Tomigaya
富ヶ谷

(1)

(2)

Jinnan
神南

Kishi Mem. Gym.
岸記念体育館

(6)

(5)

NTT Yoyogi
NTT 代々木

神山町

NHK Broadcasting Center
(Hōsō Center)放送センター

Kamiyamachō

Emb. of New Zealand
ニュージーランド大使館

Shibuya Public Hall

Shibuya Ward Office
渋谷区役所

84

Shibuya Girls' H.
渋谷女子高校

Tobu Hotel
東武ホテル

(1)

Nat'l
Childre
(Kodom)

Emb. of Mongolia
モンゴル大使館

Kanze Noh Theater
観世能楽堂

Udagawachō
宇田川町

Shibuya Parco
渋谷パルコ

Met Children's
House

50

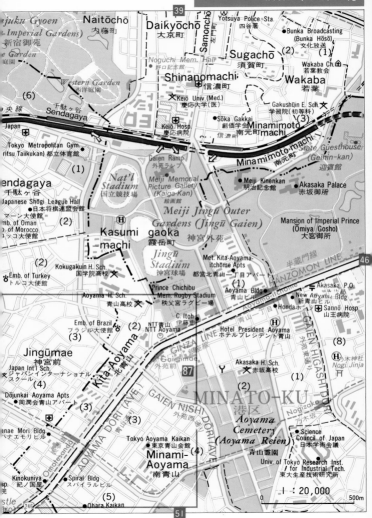

juku Gyoen Naitōchō Daikyōchō Samonchō Yotsuya Police Sta. 四谷署
Imperial Gardens) 内藤町 大京町 左門町 Bunka Broadcasting
新宿御苑 (Bunka Hōsō)
e Garden Noguchi Mem. Hall Sugachō 文化放送 (1)
庭園 野口記念館 須賀町 (2)
Western Garden Shinanomachi Wakaba Ch. ✝
西洋園 (6) 信濃町 Wakaba 若葉教会
✝ Keiō Univ. (Med.) 若葉
慶応大学(医) Gakushūin E. Sch. ✗
央線 千駄ヶ谷 Sendagaya Sōka Gakkai 学習院(初等科)(3)
Japan Keiō Hosp. 創価学会 Minamimoto
慶応病院 信濃町 南元町 machi
✝ Tokyo Metropolitan Gym. Gaien Ramp State Guesthouse
ritsu Taiikukan) 都立体育館 (1) 外苑ランプ Minamimoto-machi (Geihin-kan)
南元町 迎賓館
Sendagaya Nat'l Meiji Memorial ● Meiji Kinenkan ● Akasaka Palace
千駄ヶ谷 Stadium Picture Gallery 明治記念館 赤坂御所
Japanese Shōgi League Hall 国立競技場 (Kaiga-Kan)
●日本将棋連盟会館 絵画館 *Meiji Jingū Outer* Mansion of Imperial Prince
マーン大使館 (2) *Gardens (Jingū Gaien)* (Ōmiya Gosho)
. of Oman Kasumi gaoka 神宮外苑 大宮御所
トッコ大使館 of Morocco machi
(1) 霞岳町 *Jingū* Met. Kita-Aoyama-
Stadium itchōme Apts
(2) Kokugakuin H. Sch. 神宮球場 都営北青山一丁目アパート HANZOMON LINE
●Emb. of Turkey 国学院高校 ✗ (1) Akasaka P.O.
トルコ大使館 Aoyama Bldg 赤坂局 ●New Aoyama Bldg
Aoyama H. Sch. Prince Chichibu 青山ビル 新青山ビル
青山高校 ✗ Mem. Rugby Stadium ●Honda 本田 Sannō Hosp.
秩父宮ラグビー場 山王病院
Emb. of Brazil C. Itoh 伊藤忠 Hotel President Aoyama (8)
ブラジル大使館 (2) NTT青山 ホテルプレジデント青山
NTT Aoyama Akasaka H. Sch.
Jingūmae Gaienmae 赤坂高校 ✗ (1)
神宮前 外苑前 (2)
Japan Int'l Sch.
✗ジャパンインターナショナル Kita-Aoyama MINATO-KU
スクール (4) 北青山 港区
Dōjunkai Aoyama Apts Aoyama
●同潤会青山アパート (3) Cemetery
anae Mori Bldg (3) (Aoyama Reien) Science
ハナエモリビル Tokyo Aoyama Kaikan 青山霊園 Council of Japan
●東京青山会館 (4) 日本学術会議
Kinokuniya Minami- Univ. of Tokyo Research Inst.
●Spiral Bldg Aoyama for Industrial Tech.
紀ノ国屋 スパイラルビル 南青山 東大生産技術研究所
castle
20,000
✗ Nogi Jinja
乃木神社
●Ohara Kaikan 0 500m

GAIEN HIGASHI DORI
KITA-Aoyama
GINZA LINE 銀座線
GAIEN NISHI DORI AVE. 外苑西通り
AOYAMA DORI AVE. 青山通り
Omotesandō
87
51
39
46
45

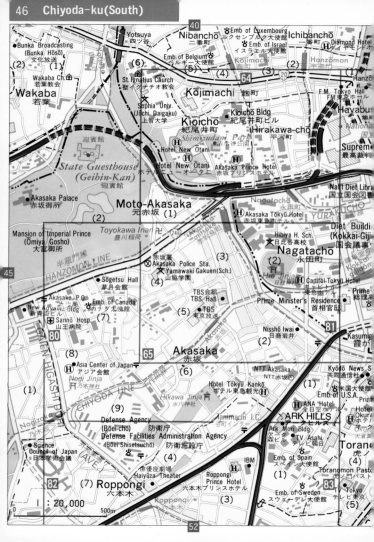

40

● Bunka Broadcasting
(Bunka Hōsō)
文化放送
(2)   (1)

Yotsuya
四ツ谷

Nibanchō
二番町

● Emb of Luxembourg
ルクセンブルク大使館

Emb. of Israel
イスラエル大使館

Ichibanchō
一番町

Diamond Hotel
ダイヤモンドH

● Wakaba Ch.
若葉教会
(6)

St. Ignatius Church
聖イグナチオ教会

Emb. of Belgium ●
ベルギー大使館
(5)   (4)

Kojimachi
麹町

(3)   20

Hanzomon
半蔵門

Hanzo

Wakaba
若葉

Sophia Univ.
(Jōchi, Daigaku)
上智大学

64

Kōjimachi
麹町

F.M. Tokyo Hall
F.M.東京ホール

Hayabu

Kioichō
紀尾井町

Kioichō Bldg
紀尾井町ビル

Hirakawa-chō
平河町

National

Shimizudani Park
清水谷公園

Suprem
最高裁

Hotel New Ōtani
ホテルニューオータニ

Hotel New Ōtani
ホテルニューオータニ

Akasaka Prince Hotel
赤坂プリンスホテル

State Guesthouse
(Geihin-Kan)
迎賓館

Nat'l Diet Libra
国立国会図書

● Akasaka Palace
赤坂御所

Moto-Akasaka
元赤坂 (1)

Nagatachō
永田町

H Akasaka Tōkyū Hotel
赤坂東急ホテル

Diet Buildi
(Kokkai-Giji
国会議事

(2)

Toyokawa Inari 卍
豊川稲荷

YURAKUCHO

Mansion of Imperial Prince
(Ōmiya/Gosho)
大宮御所

HANZOMON LINE
半蔵門線

(245)

Hibiya H. Sch.
日比谷高校

Nagatachō
永田町

Kokk

赤坂署
⊗ Akasaka Police Sta.
(3)

(2)

H Capitol Tōkyō Hotel
キャピトル東急ホテル

45

Sōgetsu Hall
草月会館

Yamawaki Gakuen(Sch.)
山脇学園
(4)

Hie Jinja
日枝神社

Prime Minister's Residence
首相官邸

Prime
総理

New Aoyama ● Bldg
新青山ビル

● Emb. of Canada
カナダ大使館
(7)

TBS会館
TBS Hall ●

81

80

● Sannō Hosp.
山王病院

(8)

(5)

● TBS
東京放送

Nisshō Iwai ●
日商岩井
(2)

Kasumi
霞ヶ

GAIEN-HIGASHI-DORI

65

Akasaka
赤坂

NTT Akasaka
NTT赤坂

Kyōdō News S
共同通信社

H Asia Center of Japan
アジア会館

Nogi Jinja
乃木神社

(6)

Emb. of U.S.A.
米国大使館

CHIYODA LINE
千代田線

Hikawa Jinja 日
氷川神社

Hotel Tōkyū Kankō
ホテル東急観光 H

(1)

Hotel Okura
ホテルオークラ

H

(1)

(9)

Defense Agency
(Bōei-chō)
防衛庁

Tanimachi I.C.
谷町インター

H ANA Hotel
全日空ホテル

ARK HILLS
アークヒルズ

ホテル

Nogizaka
乃木坂

Defense Facilities Administration Agency
(Bōei Shisetsuchō) 防衛施設庁

Ark Mori Bldg
森ビル

TV Asahi
テレビ朝日

Torane
虎ノ

● Science
Council of Japan
日本学術会議

82

(7) Roppongi
六本木

俳優座劇場
Haiyūza Theater
(4)

IBM
IBM

Roppongi
Prince Hotel
六本木プリンスホテル

Emb. of Spain
スペイン大使館

Toranomon Pasto
虎ノ門パスト
(4)

(2)

Emb. of Sweden
スウェーデン大使館

83

Tokyo
テレビ東京

1:20,000

Roppongi
六本木

(3)

(5)

500m

52

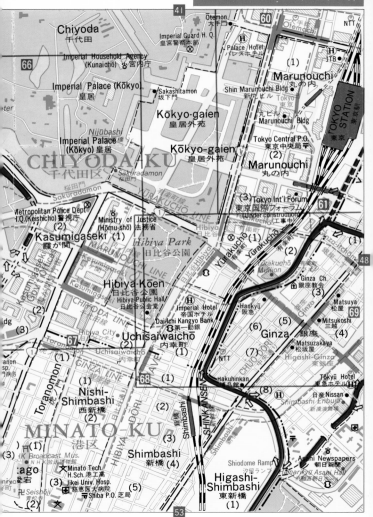

Chiyoda
千代田

Otemon
大手門

NTT

Imperial Guard H.Q.
皇宮警視本部

Palace Hotel
パレスホテル

JTB

Imperial Household Agency
(Kunaichō) 宮内庁

Marunouchi
丸の内

(1)

Shin Marunouchi Bldg
新丸ビル

Tokyo

Imperial Palace (Kōkyo)
皇居

Sakashitamon
坂下門

Marunouchi Bldg
丸ビル

TOKYO
STATION
東京駅

Kōkyo-gaien
皇居外苑

Tokyo Central P.O.
東京中央局

東京

Nijūbashi
二重橋

Marunouchi
丸の内

Imperial Palace
(Kōkyo) 皇居

Kōkyo-gaien
皇居外苑

CHIYODA-KU
千代田区

Sakuradamon
桜田門

(2)

(3) Tokyo Int'l Forum
東京国際フォーラム

(Under construction)
工事中

Sakuradamon
桜田門

YŪRAKUCHŌ LINE
有楽町線

(1)

(1)

Metropolitan Police Dept
H.Q.(Keishichō)警視庁

Ministry of Justice
法務省

Hibiya
日比谷

Yūrakuchō
有楽町

(1)

Yūrakuchō
有楽町

(1)

Kasumigaseki
霞が関

(1)

Hibiya Park
日比谷公園

(2)

Yūrakuchō
Mullion

(2)

Kasumigaseki
霞が関

MARUNOUCHI LINE

Ginza Ch.
銀座教会

(3)

Hibiya-Kōen
日比谷公園

(3)

Hibiya Public Hall
日比谷公会堂

Imperial Hotel
帝国ホテル

Hankyū
阪急

Matsuya
松屋

Mitsukoshi
三越

(4)

CHIYODA LINE

(2)

(3)

Dai-ichi Kangyo Bank
第一勧銀

(6)

(5)

Ginza
銀座

銀座

Matsuzakaya
松坂屋

Hibiya City

Uchisaiwaichō
内幸町

Matsuzakaya
松坂屋

CHUO-DORI

(2)

Toranomon
虎ノ門

Uchisaiwaichō
内幸町

(1)

NTT

Higashi-Ginza
東銀座

GINZA LINE

Hakuhinkan
博品館

(8)

Tōkyū Hotel
東急ホテル

Nishi-
Shimbashi
西新橋

Nissan
日産

Shimbashi Enbujō
新橋演舞場

MINATO-KU
港区

(2)

(1)

Shimbashi
新橋 (4)

SHINKANSEN
新幹線

NHK Broadcast Mus.
NHK放送博物館

(3)

Minato Tech.
H.Sch. 港工高

Shiodome Ramp
汐留ランプ

Asahi Newspapers
朝日新聞

ago
愛宕

(3)

Jikei Univ. Hosp.
慈恵医大病院

(5)

Higashi-
Shimbashi
東新橋
(1)

Hamarikyū Asahi Hall
浜離宮朝日ホール

Shiba P.O. 芝局

Seishoji

(2)

42

(2) 日本銀行

三越
(1) Mitsukoshi

NIHOMB
Edobashi 日

NTT

Nippon Bldg
日本ビル

Koamicho

(H) JTB

Nihombashi
(1)日本橋

Tōkyū Dept Store
東急デパート本店

Stock
Exchange
証券取引所

(1)
Marunouchi
丸の内

Tekkō Bldg
鉄鋼ビル

Tokyo
東京

Kokusai Kanko
国際観光会館
Yaesu
八重洲

'ombashi
日本橋

(2)

Kaya-
bachō
茅場町

(2)

丸ビル
Marunouchi Bldg

Daimal Dept Store
大丸デパート

Tokyo Central P.O.
東京中央〒

STATION
東京駅

Chūō Police Sta.
中央署

(3)

71

Marunouchi
丸の内

Yaesu
八重洲

(15)

Takarachō Ramp
宝町ランプ

Shinka
新

70

Kyōbashi
京橋

(3)

Tokyo Int'l Forum
東京国際フォーラム

Marunouchi Ramp
丸の内ランプ

Hatchōbori
八丁堀

(Under Constraction)
工事中

(3)

Kyōbashi Hosp.
京橋病院 ✚

47

(1)

Yūrakuchō
有楽町

(2)

(3)

(4)

Hatchōbori
八丁堀

Takahashi(Br.)
高橋

Yūrakuchō
Mullion

Kyōbashi Ramp
京橋ランプ

(1)

(1)

Mina
南海

Ginza Ch.
銀座教会

(3)

Shintomi
新富

Irifune
入船

Minato
湊

(6)

(5)

Matsuya
松屋

(3)

(2)

(3)

Ginza
銀座

Mitsukoshi
三越

Chūō Ward Office
中央区役所

NTT Tsukiji
NTT築地

Matsuzakaya
松坂屋

(4)

Tsukiji Police Sta.
築地警察署

(1)

Higashi-Ginza
東銀座

Kabuki-za
歌舞伎座

Akashicho
明石町

Tōkyū Hotel
東急ホテル

(H)

Ginza Ramp
銀座ランプ

(2)

Tsukiji Maternity Hosp.
築地産院

(8)

(H)

日産 Nissan

St. Luke's Hosp.
(Sei Roka Byōin)
聖路加病院

Shimbashi Enbujo
新橋演舞場

Kyōbashi P.O.
京橋局

(4)

(3)

Nat'l Cancer Center
国立がんセンター

Hydrographic Dept
海上保安庁水路部

Nishi Hongan-ji
(Tsukiji Branch)
西本願寺(築地別院)

Akatsuki Park
あかつき公園

(7)

(1)

Tsukiji
築地

Asahi Newspapers (Tokyo H.O.)
朝日新聞

(6)

IBM

Nichirei
ニチレイ

CHŪŌ-K
中央区

Namiyoke Jinja
波除神社

(5)
東京中央卸売市場
Tokyo Central Wholesale Market

(3)

Tsukish
月島

54

gyocho
形町
Hamachō 浜町
(3)

Hamachō ランプ

(1) **Tokiwa** 常盤 (2)

Takabashi 高橋

43
Basho Mem. Hall
●芭蕉記念館

Suitengū (Sta.)
水天宮前

(2)

Nakasu
中州

清洲橋
Kiyosu-bashi (Br.)

Kiyosumi (3)
清澄 (2)

KOTO-KU
江東区

kigaracho
蛎殻町

ngūmae
天宮前

●Tokyo City Air Terminal (Hakozaki)
東京シティエアターミナル（箱崎） 中村学園(Sch.)
Nakamura Gakuen

akozakichō
箱崎町

Kiyosumi Garden
清澄庭園

Miyoshi 三好

Hakozaki I.C.
箱崎インター

IBM

Sumidagawa-ōhashi (Br.)
隅田川大橋
(2)

(2)

(1)

Hirano (3)
平野
(2)

Eitai-bashi (Br.)
永代橋

Saga
佐賀 (1)

(1)

Fukagawa 深川

Fukuzumi Ramp
福住ランプ

(2)

m. Jr. Coll.
科短大

Fukuzumi
福住 (1)

Hōjōin
法乗院

Fuyuki
冬木

omo Twin Bldg
ツインビル

(1)

NTT Fukagawa
NTT深川

(3)

Eitai
永代
(2)

**Monzen-
nakachō**
門前仲町

深川不動 卍
Fukagawa Fudō

(2)

Tomioka Tomioka Hachimangū
富岡 富岡八幡宮

Monzen-nakachō
門前仲町

(1)

Kurofune-bashi
黒船橋

(2)

Riverpoint Tower
リバーポイントタワー
River City 21
リバーシティ21

(1) Fukagawa Sports Center
深川スポーツセンター

EITAI DORI (AVE.)
永代通り

(2)

shi Jinja
神社 (2)

Etchūjima Park
越中島公園

Botan
牡丹

ukuda
佃

Aioi-bashi (Br.)
相生橋

Furuishiba 古石場

KIYOSUMI DORI (AVE.)
清澄通り

Tokyo Univ. of
Mercantile Marine
東京商船大学

(3)

(2)

Etchūjima
越中島

(3)

(1)

Daisan Comm. H. Sch.
第三商業高校

KEIYO LINE
京葉線

1 : 20,000
500m

Toyosu-bashi (Br.)
豊洲橋

55

Nat'l Yoyogi Gymnasium
国立代々木競技場

44
86

Kishi Mem. Gym.
岸記念体育館

Dōjunkai Aoyama A
同潤会青山ア

Jinnan 神南 (2)

(6)

NHK Broadcasting Center
(Hōsō Center)放送センター

FUJI DORI (AVE.)

Hanae Mori Bldg
ハナエモリビル

(5)

神山町
Kamiyamachō

Shibuya Public Hall
渋谷公会堂

(1)

Shibuya Ward Office
渋谷区役所

H Tōbu Hotel
東武ホテル

Shibuya Girls' H. Sch.
渋谷女子高校

Aoyama Hosp.
青山病院

Kinokuniya
紀ノ国屋

Udagawachō
宇田川町

184

Kanze Noh Theater
観世能楽堂

Bunkamura
東急文化村

Shibuya Parco
渋谷パルコ

Met Children's
House

Nat'l Children's Castle
(Kodomo-no-shiro)
青山

Aoyama Theater
青山劇場

Aoyama Gakuin U
青山学院大学

(1)

Shōtō
松濤

(1)

Tōkyū Dept Store
東急本店

SHIBUYA-K
渋谷区

(2)

Seibu Dept Store
西武デパート

Dōgenzaka
道玄坂

Shibuya
渋谷

Shibuya P.O.
渋谷局

H

(2)

(2)

NTT

Maruya-
machō
円山町

Shinsen 神泉

Shinsen-
chō
神泉町

(1)

Tōhō Seimei Bldg
東邦生命ビル

Shibuya
渋谷

Tōkyū Plaza
東急プラザ

Shibuya Police Sta.
渋谷署

Konnō Hachimangu
金王八幡宮

(3)

85

SHUT

Jissen Joshi Gakue
実践女子学園

(4)

SHIN TAMAGAWA LINE
新玉川線

Tōkyū (H.Q.)
東急(本社)

Shibuya Ramp
渋谷ランプ

Sakuragaokachō
桜丘町

Emb. of Philippines
フィリピン大使館

TOYOKO LINE
東横線

YAMANOTE LINE

(1)

Nampeidaichō
南平台町

Uguisudanichō
鶯谷町

Higashi
東

(2)

Nissan Mutual
Life Insurance
日産生命

Emb. of Malaysia
マレーシア大使館

NTT The B
NTT渋谷

Daikanyamachō
代官山町

(3)

Emb. of Hungary
ハンガリー大使館

Hachiyamachō
鉢山町

Daiichi Comm. H. Sch.
第一商業高校

(2)

Aobadai
青葉台

Aoba Int'l Sch.
青葉インターナショナルスクール

Sarugakuchō
猿楽町

Ebisu-Nishi
恵比寿西

Emb. of Senegal
セネガル大使館

(1)

デンマーク大使館
Emb. of Denmark

Daikan-yama
代官山

Emb. of Egypt
エジプト大使館

(1)

MEGURO-KU
目黒区

Hillside
Terrace
ヒルサイドテラス

1 : 20,000
500m

(3) Ebisu-Minami
恵比寿南

Naka-Meguro
中目黒

(2)

Ebisu-Minami
恵比寿南

45

Defense Agency (Bōei-chō) 防衛庁

GAIEN-NISHI DORI 外苑西通り

(3)

87

Tokyo Aoyama Kaikan 東京青山会館

Minami-Aoyama 南青山

(4)

Aoyama Cemetery (Aoyama Reien) 青山霊園

Nogizaka 乃木坂

● **Science Council of Japan** 日本学術会議

Univ. of Tokyo Research Inst. for Industrial Tech. (7) 東大生産技術研究所

GAIEN-HIGASHI DORI

(9)

(4)

● 俳優座劇場 Haiyūza Theater

Roppongi 六本木

Roppongi

(5)

Ohara Kaikan 小原会館

Nezu Art Mus. 根津美術館

(2)

Jiyū Theater 自由劇場

HIBIYA LINE 日比谷線

⊗ **Azabu Police Sta.** 麻布署

(1)

(6)

WY No.3 都高速3号線

(6)

スーダン大使館 Emb. of Sudan

Takagichō Ramp 高樹町ランプ

Kōwa Int'l Bldg 興和インターナショナルビル

82

(6)

● **TV Asahi** テレビ朝日

Mansion of Prince Hitachi 常陸宮邸

of Peru ー大使館

(7)

ガーナ大使館 Emb. of Ghana

ラオス大使館 Emb. of Laos

Tax Office 税務署

(4) **Nishi-Azabu** 西麻布

Jōnan H. Sch. 城南高校

(3)

(3)

ugakuin Univ. 院大学

(3)

✕ **Tokyo Jogakukan** 東京女学館

広尾ガーデンヒルズ Hiro-o Garden Hills

Emb. of China 中国大使館

Emb. of Austria オーストリア大使館

Moto-Azabu 元麻布

52

(5)

Japan Red Cross Medical Service Center (Nisseki Iryō Center) 日赤医療センター

✕ **Junshin Joshigakuen** 頌心女子学園

Azabu H. Sch. 麻布高校

西町インターナショナルスクール Nishimachi Int'l Sch.

(1)

Hiro-o H.Sch. 広尾高校

Hiro-o 広尾 (4)

スイス大使館 Emb. of Switzerland

● **Aiiku Hosp.** 愛育病院

Emb. of Pakistan パキスタン大使館

卍 Zempuku-ji 善福寺

ノルウェー大使館 Emb. of Norway

Mormons Ch. 末日聖徒教会

Emb. of Korea 韓国大使館

(2)

✕ **Univ. of Sacred Heart** 聖心女子大学

Hiro-o 広尾

Int'l Sch. Int'l 学院

Pr. Arisugawa Mem. Park 有栖川宮記念公園

● **Tokyo Met. Central Library** 都立中央図書館

Emb. of Czechoslovakia チェコスロバキア大使館

(5)

Shoun-ji 祥雲寺

(5)

Emb. of Germany ドイツ大使館

Emb. of Finland フィンランド大使館

Minami-Azabu 南麻布

(3)

MEIJI DORI AVE. 明治通り

(4)

Emb. of France フランス大使館

Emb. of Zimbabwe ジンバブエ大使館

Emb. of Iran イラン大使館

(1)

Ebisu 恵比寿

● Hiro-o Hosp. 広尾病院 (2)

(E.Sch.) Keiō Yōchisha 慶応幼稚舎

Tengenji Ramp 天現寺ランプ

卍 Kōrin-ji 光林寺

SHUTO EXPWY No.2 首都高速2号線

(3)

Shirokane 白金

(4)

✕ **Kitasato Univ. (Pharm.)** 北里大学

(1)

Met. Mus'm of Photography 京都写真美術館

(3)

(5)

Ebisu 恵比寿

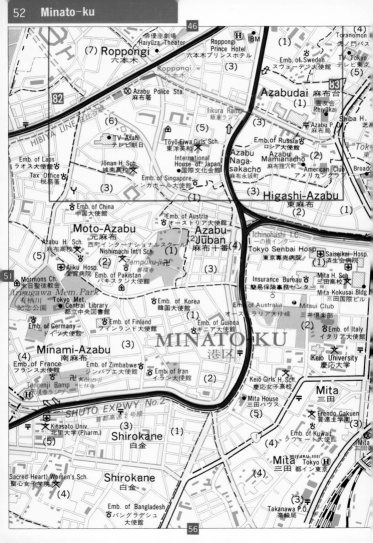

46

(7) Roppongi 六本木
俳優座劇場 Haiyūza Theater
Roppongi Prince Hotel 六本木プリンスホテル
IBM
(1)
(4) Toranomon 虎ノ門
虎ノ門バス
TV Tokyo テレビ東京 **(5)**

Emb. of Sweden スウェーデン大使館 **(1)**

82

Azabudai 麻布台
(1)
霊友会 Reiyūkai
Shiba H. 芝高

Azabu Police Sta. 麻布署

Iikura Ramp 飯倉ランプ

(6)
TV Asahi テレビ朝日
Tōyō-Eiwa Girls' Sch. 東洋英和
(5)
Emb. of Russia ロシア大使館 **(1)**
Azabu P.O. 麻布局

Jōnan H. Sch. 城南高校 **(3)**
International House of Japan 国際文化会館
Azabu Nagasakachō 麻布永坂町
Azabu Mamianachō 麻布狸穴町 **(2)**
American Club アメリカンクラブ Broado

Emb. of Laos ラオス大使館
Tax Office 税務署
Emb. of Singapore シンガポール大使館 **(1)**
(3)

Higashi-Azabu 東麻布 **(2)**
(1)

(5)
Emb. of China 中国大使館
Emb. of Austria オーストリア大使館
Ichinohashi I.C. 一の橋インタ
Tokyo Senbai Hosp. 東京専売病院
Saiseikai Hosp. 済生会病院 **(1)**

Moto-Azabu 元麻布
Azabu H. Sch. 麻布高校
Nishimachi Int'l Sch. 西町インターナショナルスクール
Azabu-Jūban 麻布十番 **(2)**
(4)
Insurance Bureau 簡易保険事務センター
Mita H. Sch. 三田高校
Mita Kokusai Bldg 三田国際ビル

(5)
Aiiku Hosp. 愛育病院 **(2)**
Zempuku-ji 善福寺卍

Mormons Ch. 末日聖徒教会
Arisugawa Mem. Park 有栖川記念公園
Tokyo Met. Central Library 都立中央図書館
Emb. of Pakistan パキスタン大使館
Emb. of Korea 韓国大使館 **(1)**
Emb. of Australia オーストラリア大使館
Mitsui Club 三井倶楽部

MINATO-KU 港区

(5)
Emb. of Germany ドイツ大使館
Emb. of Finland フィンランド大使館 **(3)**
Emb. of Guinea ギニア大使館
Emb. of Italy イタリア大使館 **(2)**

Minami-Azabu 南麻布 **(4)**
Emb. of France フランス大使館
Emb. of Zimbabwe ジンバブエ大使館
Emb. of Iran イラン大使館 **(2)**
Keio University 慶応大学

Tengenji Ramp 天現寺ランプ
Kōrin-ji 光林寺卍
Keiō Girls' H. Sch. 慶応女子高校
Mita House 三田ハウス **(5)**
Mita 三田

SHUTO EXPWY No.2 首都高速2号線 **(3)**
Frendo Gakuen 普連土学園
Kitasato Univ. 北里大学(Pharm.) (薬)
(1)
Emb. of Kuwait クウェート大使館 **(4)**

(5)
Shirokane 白金

Sacred Heart Women's Sch. 聖心女子学院
(4)
Shirokane 白金
Mita 三田
miyako Hotel 都イン東京 **(4)**
Mita Tokyo 三田 都イン東京
Mita 三田

Emb. of Bangladesh バングラデシュ大使館
Takanawa P.O. 高輪局 **(3)**

56

47

Shimbashi
新橋(4)

Higashi-Shimbashi
東新橋
(1)

Shiodome Ramp
汐留ランプ

Hankyū Asahi Hall
阪急朝日

(1) (3) HK Broadcast Mus.
NHK 放送博物館

Atago
愛宕

Minato Tech
H.Sch.港工高

(3) Jikei Univ. Hosp.
慈恵医大病院

Shiba P.O. 芝局

(2) Jikei Med. Univ.
東京慈恵医大
(6)

Nether
ンダ大使館

Ondmon
御成門

Seisho-ji
正眼寺

(3)

Seiso
Gakui

Tokyo Prince Hotel
東京プリンスホテル

(H) **Shiba-Kōen**
芝公園

Atago Police Sta.
愛宕警察

Japan Red Cross
(Nippon Sekijujisha)
日本赤十字社

Kyoritsu
Coll. of Pharm.
共立薬科大
(1)

Hamamatsu-chō

Minato Ward Office
港区役所
(1)

(2)

Shiba-
Daimon

Shiba-
Daijingū
芝大神宮

(1)

**Hama Detached
Palace Garden
(Hama Rikyū Teien)**
浜離宮恩賜庭園

Shiba Comm.H.Sch.
芝商業高校

Hamamatsuchō
浜松町
Kyu-
Shibarikyū
Garden
旧芝離宮
恩賜庭園

Tokyo Trade Center
東京産業貿易会館

**Shiba
Park**
芝公園

(2)

World Trade
Center Bldg
世界貿易センタービル

(4)

(4)

ub. of Chile
大使館

Shiba-kō-en
Ramp
芝公園ランプ

Shiba
芝

(2)

(1)

(2)

Tokyo bus Bldg
東京 ビル

(1)

Takeshiba
Passenger Terminal
竹芝旅客ターミナル

(1)

Hamazakibashi I.C.
浜崎橋インター

Water-bus Station
水上バスのりば

(3)

NEC
本電気

(5)

(4)

Tōshiba Bldg.
東芝ビル

Kaigan
海岸

(1)

(2)

54

Port of Tokyo
(Tokyo-ko)
東京港

Hinode Sanbashi (pier)
日の出桟橋

TOKYO MONORAIL
東京モノレール

machi 田町

Minato
Ward
Sports Center
スポーツセンター

Shibaura
芝浦

(2)

(2)

(3)

Shibaura Inst. of Tech.
芝浦工業大

Shibaura
芝浦

(3)

(2)

Futo Park
埠頭公園

Kaigan
海岸

1 : 20,000

500m

58

an Times
タイムズ

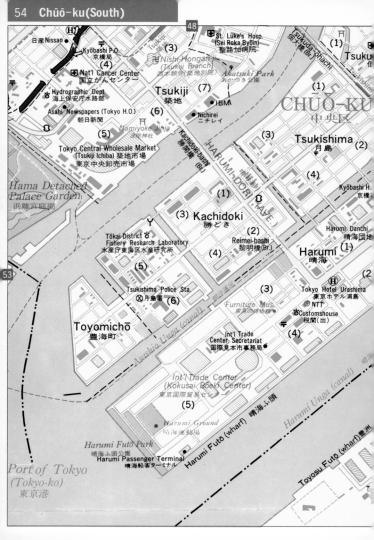

日産 Nissan

(H)

Kyōbashi P.O.
京橋局
(4)

Nat'l Cancer Center
国立がんセンター

Hydrographic Dept
海上保安庁水路部

Asahi Newspapers (Tokyo H.O.)
朝日新聞

(5)

Namiyoke Jinja
波除神社

Tokyo Central Wholesale Market
(Tsukiji Ichiba) 築地市場
東京中央卸売市場

48

(3)

Nishi-Hongan-ji
(Tsukiji Branch)
西本願寺築地別院

Tsukiji
築地
(7)

(6)

St. Luke's Hosp.
(Sei Roka Byōin)
聖路加病院

Akatsuki Park
あかつき公園

IBM

Nichirei
ニチレイ

Tsukuda Ōhachi
佃大橋 (Br.)

Tsuku
佃

(1)   (1)

CHŪŌ-KU
中央区

(1)

(1)

Tsukishima
月島
(2)

(3)

Hama Detached
Palace Garden
浜離宮庭園

Kachidoki-bashi
勝鬨橋 (Br.)

HARUMI-DŌRI AVE.

(1)

(3) Kachidoki
勝どき

Tōkai District
Fishery Research Laboratory
水産庁東海区水産研究所

(5)

(2)

Reimei-bashi
黎明橋 (Br.)

(4)

(4)

Kyōbashi H.
京橋

Harumi Danchi
晴海団地

Harumi
晴海
(1)

(2)

53

Tsukishima Police Sta.
月島署
(6)

(3)

Tokyo Hotel Urashima
東京ホテル浦島

NTT

Customshouse
税関 (出)

(4)

Toyomichō
豊海町

Furniture Mus.
家具の博物館

Asashio Unga (canal)

Int'l Trade
Center Secretariat
国際見本市事務局

Int'l Trade Center
(Kokusai Bōeki Center)
東京国際貿易セ

(5)

Harumi Ground
晴海運動場

Harumi Futō (wharf) 晴海ふ頭

Harumi Unga (canal)

Toyosu Futō (wharf) 豊洲

Harumi Futō Park
晴海ふ頭公園

Harumi Passenger Terminal
晴海船客ターミナル

Harumi Futō (wharf) 晴海ふ頭

Port of Tokyo
(Tokyo-ko)
東京港

49

Aioi-bashi (Br.)
相生橋

Tokyo Univ. of
Mercantile Marine
東京商船大学

Etchūjima
越中島

KEIYŌ LINE
京葉線

Daisan Comm.H.Sch.
第三商業高校

Toyosu-bashi
豊洲橋

Hamazono-
bashi
浜園橋

(1)

Kaname-
bashi (Br.)
鎹橋

Edagawa Ramp
枝川ランプ

Commercial Jr. Coll.
都立商科短大
bashi Com. H.Sch.
京橋商業高校

(1)

Harumi-bashi (Br.)
晴海橋

HARUMI DORI

Ishikawajima-Harima
Heavy Industries
石川島播磨重工業

(3)

Asanagi-bashi (Br.)
朝凪橋

Edagawa
枝川

(2)

(2)

Tomoegumi Ironworks
巴組鉄工

(1)

Ishikawajima-Harima
Heavy Industries
石川島播磨重工業

Nisshin Sugar
日新製糖

Toyosu Park
豊洲公園

(4)

Shōwa Univ. Toyosu Hosp.
昭和大付属豊洲病院

Toyosu-yonchōme Danchi (Apts)
豊洲4丁目団地

Toyosu (5)
豊洲

Shinonome-bashi (Br.)
東雲橋

Tatsumi-bashi (Br.)
辰巳橋

Shin-Tokyo Thermoelectric Power Plant
東電新東京火力発電所

Kōtō Hosp.
江東病院

Shinonome
東雲

Mitsubishi Steel
三菱製鋼

(1)

(6)

Toyosu Plant
豊洲工場

1 : 20,000

500m

MINATO-KU 港区

Shirokane 白金

Emb. of Bangladesh バングラデシュ大使館

Miyako Hotel 都ホテル東京

Meiji Gakuin Univ. 明治学院大学

Happoen 八芳園

Seishin (Sacred Heart) Women's Sch 聖心女子学院 (4)

Inst. of Public Health 国立公衆衛生院

Shirokanedai 白金台

Inst. of Medical Science 東京大学医科学研究所

NTT Shirokane NTT白金

Shōei Joshi Gakuin 頌栄女子学院

Teishin Hosp. 逓信病院

Emb. of Somalia ソマリア大使館

Eight Buddhist Temples of Osaki 卍大崎八ヶ寺

Hatakeyama Collection 畠山記念館

Emb. of Indonesia インドネシア大使館

Higashi-Gotanda 東五反田

Univ. of Tokyo Inst. for Educational Research 東京都教育研究所

Met. Teien Art Musm 東京都庭園美術館

Meguro Ramp

SHUTO EXPWY No.2 首都高速2号線

NTT

Nat'l Park for Nature Study 国立自然教育園

Ebisu 恵比寿

Tokyo Met. Musm of Photography 東京都写真美術館

Sapporo Breweries サッポロビール

Nat'l Inst. of Health 国立予防衛生研究所

Sugino Koru 杉野コル

Kami-Ōsaki 上大崎

Emb. of Colombia コロンビア大使館

Emb. of Thailand タイ王国大使館

Dai Nippon Printing 大日本印刷 (3)

Ebisu-Minami 恵比寿南

Shibuya 渋谷

YAMANOTE LINE 山手線

Meguro 目黒

Gajōen 雅叙園

Costume Musm

Sugino Women's Coll 杉野女子大学

朝鮮第七初中級学校

Mita 三田

Kōsei Chūō Hosp. 厚生中央病院

Met. Inst. for Educational Research 都立教育研究所

Hinode Joshi Gakuen 日出女子学園

Tōkyū Store 東急ストア

MEGURO-KU 目黒区

Dai-Meguro 大目黒

YAMATE DŌRI 山手通り

Defense Agency 防衛庁

Technical Research & Development Inst. 防衛技術研究所

Emb. of Poland ポーランド大使館

Meguro Musm of Art 目黒区美術館

Meguro Ch. 目黒

Ōtori Jinja 大鳥神社

Meguro Parasitological Musm 目黒寄生虫館

Gotenyama-Rakan-ji 卍五百羅漢寺

Meguro Fudō 目黒不動

Meguro Police Sta. 目黒警察署

Nakameguro Ch. 中目黒教会

Meguro Gakuen (Sch.) 目黒学園

Shimo-Meguro 下目黒

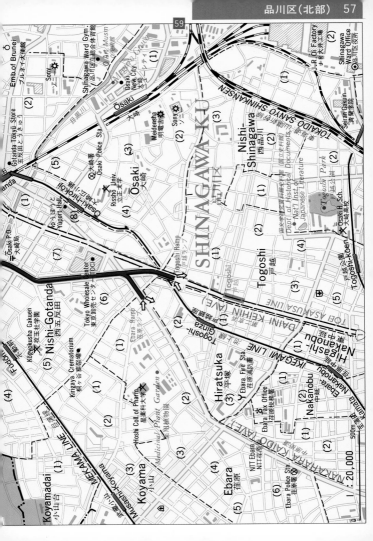

芝浦ふ頭
Shibaura Futō (wharf)

Shinagawa Futō (wharf)
品川

Kaigan 海岸 (3)

Water Police Sta. 水上警察署
水上警察署

Tokyo Customshouse 東京税関

(5)

Ground Self-Defense Force Post 陸上自衛隊芝浦分屯地

(2)

Shibaura Ramp 芝浦ランプ

Kōnan-Ōhashi (Br.) 港南大橋

53

Goshiki-bashi 五色橋
Kōei-bashi (Br.) 港栄橋

Shibaura Inst. of Tech. 芝浦工業大学
Shibaura 芝浦 (3)

Old Electric Industry 沖電気工業
Japan Times ジャパンタイムズ

Funazu-bashi (Br.) フナ頭橋
Takahama-bashi (Br.) 高浜橋

Kōnan Danchi (Apts) 港南団地 (4)

(3)

Shibaura-bashi (Br.) 芝浦橋
Takahama-bashi (Br.) 高浜橋

(4)

Shin-Kōnan-bashi (Br.) 新港南橋

Sewage Disposal Plant 下水処理場 (1)

Sony ソニー

NTT Shinagawa Twins NTT品川ツインズ
Tokyo Newspaper Co. 東京新聞社

Kōnan 港南

(2)

TOKAIDO-SAN'YO SHINKANSEN 東海道・山陽新幹線

KEIHIN-TOHOKU LINE 京浜東北線

Mita 三田
Minato-ku P.O. 港区役所
Miyako Inn (H) Tokyo 都ホテル東京
(3) 三☲

MINATO-KU 港区

Takanawa P.O. 高輪局

Hotel Town ホテルタウン (H)

Sengaku-ji 泉岳寺
Sengaku-ji (Temple) 泉岳寺 (2)

Shinagawa 品川

52

Residence of Prince Takamatsu 高松宮邸
(4)

(H) Hotel Takanawa ホテル高輪
Takanawa Gakuen 高輪学園
高輪学園

Shirokane 白金

(1)

Takanawa 高輪

Tōzen-ji 東善寺 卍

(3)

Tōkai Jr. Coll. 東海大
Takanawa Police Sta. 高輪警察署

Takanawa Prince Hotel 高輪プリンスホテル (H)

Hotel Pacific Tokyo ホテルパシフィック東京 (H)
Wing Takanawa ウイング高輪

New Takanawa Prince Hotel 新高輪プリンスホテル
Tobu Hotel 東武ホテル (H)

Ice Arena Skating Center アイスアリーナスケートセンター

SAKURADA DŌRI (AVE.) 桜田通り

56

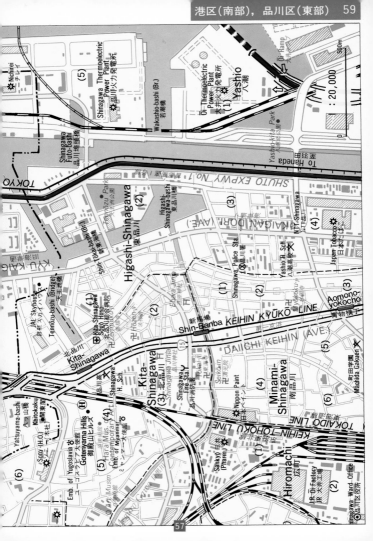

✿ Nichirei
ニチレイ

(5)

Shinagawa Thermoelectric Power Plant
品川火力発電所

☼ Thermoelectric
Power Plant
大井火力発電所
(1)

Yashio
八潮

: 20,000

Wakashio-bashi (Br.)
若潮橋

Oi Ramp
大井

Yashio-Kita Park
八潮北公園

To Haneda
至羽田

Shinagawa
Futo-bashi
品川埠頭橋

500m

TOKYO

SHUTO EXPWY No.1
首都高速１号

KAIGAN DORI (AVE.)
海岸通り

Higashi-Shinagawa
東品川

(2)

Kyuzu Park
京浜公園

Higashi
Shinagawa-bashi
東品川橋

(3)

NTT Shinagawa

Japan Tobacco
日本たばこ
(4)

Yashio H. Sch.
八潮高校 ✕

Shinagawa Police Sta.
品川警察署 ⊗

Shinagawa H. Sch.
品川高校 ✕

(1)

(2)

KYU-KAIG

JAL Skyhouse
日航スカイハウス ☼

Tennozu-bashi (Bridge)
天王洲橋

Shin Tokai-bashi (Br.)
新東海橋

(1)

Ebara Jinja
荏原神社 卍

Shinagawa
Sogo Hosp.
北品川総合病院 ⊞

Kita-
Shinagawa

(2)

Hazehi-
橋

Shin-Banba
新馬場

KEIHIN KYUKO LINE
京浜急行

Aomono-
yokocho
青物横丁

(3)

Kita-
Shinagawa
北品川

Kainokaku
☼

Yatsuyama-bashi
八ツ山橋

Sony (H.O.)
ソニー本社

(6)

Hara Mus. (4)
原美術館 ☼

Gotenyama Hills
御殿山ヒルズ
(5)

Emb. of Yugoslavia
☼ 旧ユーゴスラビア大使館

Ⓗ

Emb. of Myanmar
ミャンマー大使館 ☼

☼ Art Musm
☼ 学習院女子

Shinagawa-ku
品川区役所 ⊗

Shinagawa
H. Sch.
品川高校 ✕

(3)

Kita-Shinagawa
北品川 ⊗

Shinagawa Jima
Fire Sta.
品川消防署

DAIICHI KEIHIN (AVE.)
第一京浜

SeikiGun
誓教寺 卍

Nippon Paint
日本ペイント

(4)

Minami-
Shinagawa
南品川

(6)

(5)

KEIHIN-TOHOKU LINE

Sankyo
☼ (Pharm)
三共

TOKAIDO LINE
東海道本線

KEIHIN-TOHOKU LINE

(1)

Hiromachi
広町

J.R. Oi Factory
JR 大井工場

(2)

Maachida Gakuen ✕
校学田聖 ✕
(5)

(6)

57

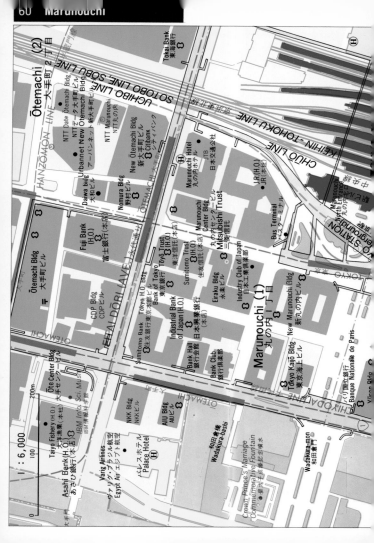

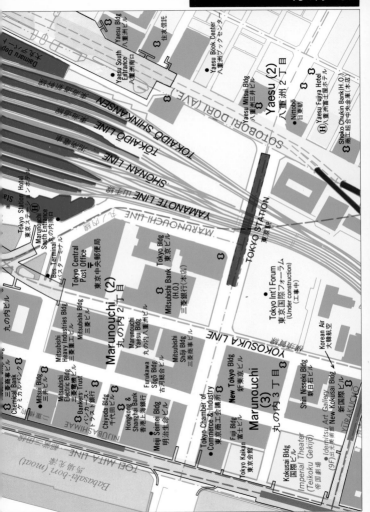

Daimaru Dep. 大丸デパート

八重洲ブックセンター Yaesu Book Center

Yaesu Bldg 八重洲ビル

住友信託 住友信託

Yaesu South Entrance 八重洲南口

Yaesu (2) 八重洲2丁目

Yaesu Mitsui Bldg 八重洲三井ビル

Nittobo 日東紡

Yaesu Fujiya Hotel 八重洲富士屋ホテル

(H) Shoko Chukin Bank(H.O.) 商工組合中央金庫(本店)

SOTOBORI DORI AVE. 外濠通り

TOKAIDO SHINKANSEN 東海道新幹線

TOKAIDO LINE 東海道線

SHONAN LINE 湘南線

YAMANOTE LINE 山手線

MARUNOUCHI LINE 丸ノ内線

TOKYO STATION 東京駅

Tokyo Station Hotel 東京ステーションホテル

(H) Marunouchi South Entrance 丸の内南口

Bus Terminal バスターミナル

Tokyo Central Post Office 東京中央郵便局

Tokyo Bldg 東京ビル

Mitsubishi Bank (H.O.) 三菱銀行(本店)

Tokyo Int'l Forum 東京国際フォーラム (Under construction) (工事中)

Korean Air 大韓航空

Marunouchi (2) 丸の内2丁目

丸の内ビル

Mitsubishi Heavy Industries Bldg 三菱重工ビル

Mitsubishi Bldg 三菱ビル

Marunouchi Yaesu Bldg 丸の内八重洲ビル

Mitsubishi Shoji Bldg 三菱商事ビル

YOKOSUKA LINE 横須賀線

三菱商事ビル Cosmo Bank コスモバンク

Mitsui Bldg 三井ビル

Mitsubishi Electric Bldg 三菱電機ビル

Bankers' Trust バンカーストラスト銀行

Chiyoda Bldg 千代田ビル

Hongkong & Shanghai Bank 香港上海銀行

Furukawa Sogo Bldg 古河総合ビル

Meiji Seimei Bldg 明治生命館

New Tokyo Bldg 新東京ビル

Shin Nisseki Bldg 新日石ビル

Shin Kokusai Bldg 新国際ビル

Marunouchi (3) 丸の内3丁目

Tokyo Chamber of Commerce & Industry 東京商工会議所

Fuji Bldg 富士ビル

Tokyo Kaikan 東京会館

Kokusai Bldg 国際ビル

Imperial Theater (Teikoku Gekijo) 帝国劇場

(97) Idemitsu Art Gallery 出光美術館

New Kokusai Bldg 新国際ビル

Babasaki-bori (moat) 馬場先濠

TOEI MITA LINE 都営三田線

Mainichi Newspapers
毎日新聞

Marubeni (H.O.)
丸紅本社

Export-Import Bank of Japan
日本輸出入銀行

Takebashi Kaikan
竹橋会館

Kanda-Nishikichō
神田錦町

Kandabashi Ran
神田橋ランプ

TAKEBASHI 竹橋

SHUTO EXPWY LOOP LINE

Ōte-bori (moat)
大手濠

Meteorological Agency
気象庁

Bronze Statue of Kiyomaro Wake
和気清麻呂像

NO.3

Common Gov't Bldgs
合同庁舎

Tokyo Fire Dept
東京消防庁

NO.2

Marunouchi Fire Sta.
丸の内消防署

NO.1

Tokyo Immigration Bureau
東京入国管理局

Japan Development
日本開発銀

Gov't Publication Service Center
大手町政府刊行物サービスセンター

Chiyoda
千代田

East Imperial Garden
(Kōkyo Higashi Gyoen)
皇居東御苑

Mitsui Bussan Bldg
三井物産ビル

Mitsui Mutual Life Insurance
三井生命(H.O.)
(本社)

KD L
国際電

Hill of Masakado's Head
(Masakado Kubizuka) 将門首塚

Ōtemachi (1)
大手町一丁目

Long-Term Credit Bank of Japan
日本長期信用銀行

Yomiu
Newspa
読売新

Hosp. of Imperial Household Agency
宮内庁病院

Sanwa Bank
三和銀行

Imperial Guard Sch.
皇宮警察学校

Ōtem
大

Site of Edo Castle
江戸城跡

Ōteman
大手門

Taiyo Fishery (H.O.)
大洋漁業(本社)

Ōte Center Bldg
大手センタービル

OTEMACHI

Cabinet Library
(Naikaku Bunko)
内閣文庫

Asahi Bank (H.O.)
あさひ銀行(本店)

IBM Info. Sci. Mus.
IBM情報科学館

CDP Bldg
CDPビル

Imperial Guard H.Q.
皇宮警察本部

Varig Airlines
ヴァリグ・ブラジル航空

Egypt Air エジプト航空

NKK Bldg
NKKビル

EIAI DŌRI

Sumitomo Bank
住友銀行東京本部ビ
Tokyo H.C
Bank of
東京

Kikyo-bori (moat)
桔梗濠

Palace Hotel
パレスホテル

AIU Bldg
AIUビル

Industrial Bank of Japan (H.O.)
日本興業銀行
(本店)

Imperial Guard H.Q.
皇宮警察本部

Bank Hall
銀行会館

Kikyōmon
桔梗門

Wadakura-bashi
和田倉橋

Bank Club
銀行倶楽部

Eiraku
永楽

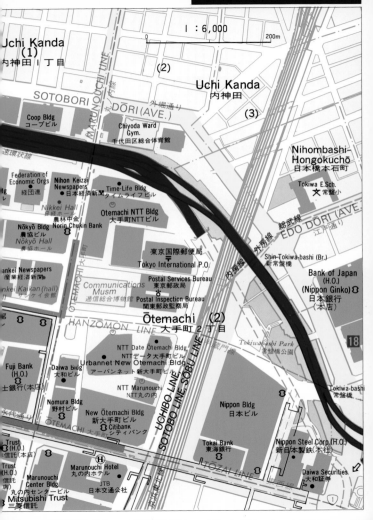

1 : 6,000

0   200m

Uchi Kanda
(1)
内神田1丁目

(2)

Uchi Kanda
内神田

(3)

SOTOBORI DORI (AVE.)
外堀通り

Coop Bldg
コープビル

Chiyoda Ward
Gym.
千代田区総合体育館

Nihombashi-
Hongokuchō
日本橋本石町

Tokiwa E.Sch.
文 常盤小

Federation of
Economic Orgs
経団連
レ

Nihon Keizai
Newspapers
日本経済新聞

Time-Life Bldg
タイムライフビル

EDO DŌRI (AVE
江戸通り

Nikkei Hall
日経ホール

Otemachi NTT Bldg
大手町NTTビル

Nōkyō Bldg
農協ビル
Nōkyō Hall
農協ホール

Norin Chukin Bank
農林中金

東京国際郵便局
Tokyo International P.O.

Shin-Tokiwa-bashi (Br.)
新常盤橋

ankei Newspapers
産業経済新聞
nkei Kaikan (hall)
サンケイ会館

Communications
Musm
通信総合博物館

Postal Services Bureau
東京郵政局
Postal Inspection Bureau
関東郵政監察局

Bank of Japan
(H.O.)
(Nippon Ginko)
日本銀行
(本店)

Ōtemachi (2)
大手町2丁目

HANZŌMON LINE

Tokiwabashi Park
常盤橋公園

18

NTT Date Ōtemachi Bldg
NTTデータ大手町ビル
Urbannet New Ōtemachi Bldg
アーバンネット新大手町ビル

Fuji Bank
(H.O.)
士銀行(本店)

Daiwa bldg
大和ビル

NTT Marunouchi
NTT丸の内

Tokiwa-bashi
常盤橋

Nomura Bldg
野村ビル

New Ōtemachi Bldg
新大手町ビル

Nippon Bldg
日本ビル

Citibank
シティバンク

水
Trust
(H.O.)
信託(本店)

ŌTEMACHI

Tokai Bank
東海銀行

Nippon Steel Corp.(H.O.)
新日本製鉄(本社)

Trust
(H.O.)
信託(本店)

Marunouchi
Center Bldg
丸の内センタービル

Marunouchi Hotel
丸の内ホテル

JTB
日本交通公社

Daiwa Securities
大和証券

TOZAI LINE

Mitsubishi Trust
三菱信託

1

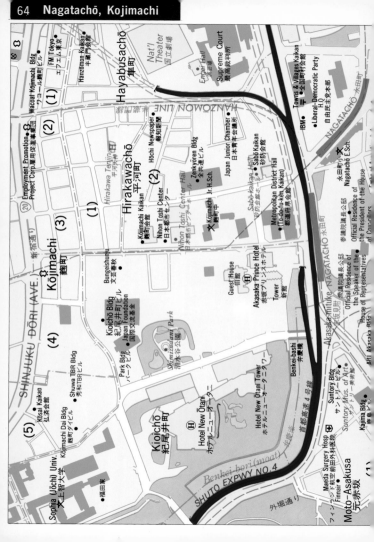

63 & 8

FM Tokyo
エフエム東京

Wacoal Kojimachi Bldg
ワコール麹町ビル

Hanzōmon Kaikan
半蔵門会館

Nat'l Theater
国立劇場

Engei Hall
演芸場

Supreme Court
最高裁判所

Towns & Villages Kaikan
全国町村会館

HANZOMON LINE

● Liberal-Democratic Party
H·Q
自由民主党本部

● IBM

NAGATACHO　永田町

(20) Employment Promotion
Project Corp.
雇用促進事業団

(2)

(1)

Hōchi Newspaper
報知新聞

Hayabusachō
隼町

Zenkyōren Bldg
全共連ビル

Sabō Kaikan
砂防会館

Japan Junior Chamber
日本青年会議所

Hirakawa Tenjin
平河天神

Hirakawachō
平河町

(2)

Kojimachi Kaikan
麹町会館

Nihon Toshi Center
日本都市センター

Nihon Toshi Center Hall
日本都市センターホール

Metropolitan District Hall
(To-do-fu-ken, Kaikan)
都道府県会館

Kojimachi Jr. H.Sch.
麹町中

(1)

(3)

Kojimachi
麹町

(1)

Bungeishunju
文芸春秋

Guest House
(別館)

Akasaka Prince Hotel
赤坂プリンスホテル

Tower
新館

Akasaka-mitsuke　NAGATACHO

Official Residence of
the Speaker of the
House of Representatives
衆議院議長公邸

Official Residence of
the President of the House
of Councilors
参議院議長公邸

SHINJUKU DŌRI (AVE.) 新宿通り

Kosai Kaikan
弘済会館

Shuwa TBR Bldg
秀和TBRビル

Kojimachi Dai Bldg
麹町ダイビル

(4)

(5)

Sophia (Jōchi) Univ.
上智大学

● Fukuda-ke
福田家

Kioichō Bldg
紀尾井町ビル

Park Bldg
パークビル

Japan Foundation
国際交流基金

Kioichō
紀尾井町

Shimizudani Park
清水谷公園

Benkei-bashi
弁慶橋

Hotel New Ōtani
ホテルニューオータニ

Hotel New Ōtani Tower
ホテルニューオータニタワー

Suntory Bldg
サントリービル

Suntory Mus. of Art
サントリー美術館

Kajima Bldg
鹿島ビル

Benkei-bori (moat)
弁慶堀

SHUTO EXPWY NO.4
首都高速4号線

Maeda Surgery Hosp
前田整形外科医院

フィンエアー日本航空営業所
Finnair

Atl'Masaka-Rido

Moto-Asakusa
元赤坂

外堀通り

(1)

House of Councillors
参議院議員会館

Nagatachō
永田町

Bldg two Members' Office
House of Representatives
衆議院第二議員会館

Bldg one Members' Office
House of Representatives
衆議院第一議員会館

KOKKAI-GIJIDOMAE
国会議事堂前

Prime Minister's
Official Residence
首相官邸

Tokyo Isuzu Motor
東京いすゞ

Science Bldg
サイエンスビル

Sabena Airlines
サベナ航空

Toshiba EM
東芝EM

GINZA LINE
銀座線

Capitol Tokyu Hotel
キャピトル東急ホテル

Hie Jinja (shrine)
日枝神社

Saam Grand Bldg
山王グランドビル

Flying Tiger Line
フライングタイガー航空

Continental Airlines
コンチネンタル航空

Philippine Airlines
フィリピン航空

メキシコ大使館

Hibiya H. Sch.
日比谷高校

Hoshigaoka Bldg
星が岡ビル

Komatsu Bldg
小松ビル

Sanō Hatten
山王飯店

Saannōshita
山王下

Yachiyo Bldg
八千代ビル

Petroleum Communication
Center 石油会館

Kokusai Akasaka Bldg
国際赤坂ビル

Nisshō Iwai
日商岩井

ASAKASA-MITSUKE
赤坂見附

(3)

Sumitomo Seimei
Akasaka Bldg
住友生命赤坂ビル

Iragi Airways
イラク航空

Kokusai Sannō Bldg
国際山王ビル

Sanya Akasaka Bldg
サンヨー赤坂ビル

East Bldg 東館
Kokusai Shin Akasaka Bldgs
国際新赤坂ビル
West Bldg 西館

AKASAKA
赤坂

HITOTSUGI DORI
一ツ木通り

TBS Kaikan
TBS会館

TBS Hall
TBSホール

Akasaka-fudōson
赤坂不動尊

Fuji Bank
富士銀行

Akasaka E. Sch.
赤坂小

虎島

Jōdo-ji
浄土寺

Jōgen-ji
净厳寺

TBS
東京放送

MINATO-KU

Akasaka
赤坂

Minato Shinkin Bank (H.O.)
港信用金(本店)

AOYAMA-DORI
青山通り

Toyokawa Inari
豊川稲荷

Toraya
虎屋

Yamawaki Gakuen (Sch.)
山脇学園

Akasaka Police Sta.
赤坂署

Entsū-ji
円通寺

TBS Golf Studio
TBSゴルフスタジオ

Akasaka Shinjuku Hotel
赤坂シャンピアホテル

1 : 8,000

0   200m

渋谷

Imperial Household Agency 宮内庁

Nijūbashi-bori (moat) 二重橋濠

Shimp-Dōkan-bori (moat) 新道灌濠

Imperial Palace 皇居

New Palace 新宮殿

Fushimi-yagura (turret) 伏見櫓

Nijūbashi (bridge) 二重橋

Sakurada-mot 桜田門

Gaisen-hori (moat) 凱旋濠

Kami-Dōkan-bori (moat) 上道灌濠

Fukiage Imperial Gardens 吹上御苑

Three Shrines in the Imperial Court 宮中三殿

Biology Laboratory 生物学研究所

Sakurada-mon 桜田門

Sakurada-bori (moat) 桜田濠

首都高速都心環状線 SHUHO EXPWY LOOP LINE

1 : 8,000

0   200m

Hanzō-mon (gate) 半蔵門

Tōjō Kaikan 東条会館

Hanzōmon 半蔵門

CHIYODA-KU 千代田区

Miyakezaka 三宅坂

UCHIBORI DORI (AVE.) 内堀通り

(246)

Supreme Court 最高裁判所

Socialist Party of Japan H.Q. 日本社会党本部

National Diet Library 国立国会図書館

Parliamentary Mus. 憲政記念館

YŪRAKUCHŌ LINE 有楽町線

Hibiya Park 日比谷公園

Hibiya Public Hall 日比谷公会堂

川 Press 川プレス

Hibiya City 日比谷シティ

Ministry of Justice 法務省

法曹会館

法務署

Public Prosecutor's Office 検察庁

Ministry of Health & Welfare 厚生省

Ministry of Labor 労働省

Environment Agency 環境庁

Nat'l Land Agency 国土庁

都立日比谷図書館
Met. Hibiya Library

Nippon Press Center 日本プレスセンター

Iino Bldg 飯野ビル
Iino Hall イイノ・ホール

Hibiya Kokusai Bldg 日比谷国際ビル

Hibiya Public Library 日比谷公会堂図書館

Tokyo High Court 東京高等裁判所

Tokyo District Court 東京地方裁判所

Ministry of Agriculture, Forestry & Fisheries 農林水産省

Tokyo Family Court 東京家裁

国際交流特物センター
Education Service Center

Tokyo Intersia Center

Ministry of Int'l Trade & Industry 通商産業省

Tokyo Expwy-Public Corp. 首都高速道路公団

Ministry of Posts & Telecommunications 郵政省

Diamond Sha ダイヤモンド社

Tōtō 東陶

Ministry of Construction 建設省

Nat'l Police Agency 警察庁

Ministry of Transport 運輸省

Ministry of Home Affairs 自治省

Maritime Safety Agency 海上保安庁

Fire Defense Agency 消防庁

Nat'l Personnel Authority 人事院

Ministry of Foreign Affairs 外務省

Science & Technology Agency 科学技術庁

Kasumigaseki 霞が関

KASUMIGASEKI

Ministry of Finance 大蔵省

No.4 Common Govt Bldg 合同庁舎

Hokkaido Develop. Agency 北海道開発庁

Garuda Airways ガルーダ・インドネシア航空

Biman Bangladesh Airlines バングラデシュ航空

UTA Airline UTA フランス航空

会計検査院
Board of Audit

Ministry of Education 文部省

Nat'l Education Center 国立教育会館

Kasumigaseki Bldg 霞が関ビル

Tokyo Club Bldg 東京倶楽部ビル

Lufthansa Airlines ルフトハンザ・ドイツ航空

Alitalia アリタリア航空

Air Nauru エアーナウル

House of Councillors 参議院

National Diet Building (Kokkai Gijidō) 国会議事堂

House of Representatives (Shugi-in) 衆議院

Kasumigaseki Ramp 霞ヶ関ランプ

Kasumigaseki Ban 霞が関ランプ

代官坂

MARUNOUCHI LINE 丸ノ内線

CHIYODA LINE 千代田線

HIBIYA LINE

TORANOMON 虎ノ門

TORANOMON LINE

SAKURADA DORI AVE. 桜田通り

Diet Press Center 国会記者会館

Prime Minister's Office 総理官邸

Okinawa Develop. Agency 沖縄開発庁

New-Kasumigaseki Bldg 新霞が関ビル

Patent Office 特許庁

Iran Air イラン航空 日本エア・システム

NCR Japan

Air Nauru エアーナウル

Tokyo 東京俱楽部ビル

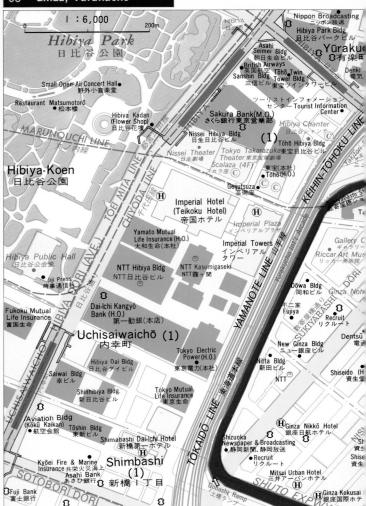

1 : 6,000
200m

Hibiya Park
日比谷公園

Nippon Broadcasting
ニッポン放送

Hibiya Park Bldg
日比谷パークビル

Yūraku
有楽町

Denki
電気

Asahi
Seimei Bldg
朝日生命ビル

British Airways
英国航空
Sanshin Bldg
三信ビル

Tōhō Twin
Tower Bldg
東宝ツインタワービル

Small Open-Air Concert Hall
野外小音楽堂

Restaurant Matsumotorō
松本楼

ツーリストインフォメーション
センター Tourist Information
Center

Hibiya Kadan
(Flower Shop)
日比谷花壇

Sakura Bank(M.O.)
さくら銀行東京営業部

Hibiya Chanter
日比谷シャンテ

MARUNOUCHI LINE
丸ノ内線

Nissei Hibiya Bldg
日生日比谷ビル

Tōhō Hibiya Bldg

(1)

Hibiya-Koen
日比谷公園

Nissei Theater
日生劇場

Tokyo Takarazuka東宝日比谷ビル
Theater東京宝塚劇場
Scalaza (4FY)
スカラ座 ⓒ

東宝(本社)
Tōhō (H.O.)

TOEI MITA LINE
都営三田線

CHIYODA LINE
千代田線

Geijutsuza
芸術座

ⓒ

KEIHIN–TOHOKU LINE

Imperial Hotel
(Teikoku Hotel)
帝国ホテル

ⓗ

Imperial Plaza
インペリアルプラザ

Imperial Towers山手線
インペリアル
タワー

Gallery C
ギャラリー C

Riccar Art Mus
リッカー美術館

Yamato Mutual
Life Insurance (H.O.)
大和生命(本社)

HIBIYA DORI (AVE.)
日比谷通り

Hibiya Public Hall
日比谷公会堂

NTT Hibiya Bldg
NTT日比谷ビル

NTT Kasumigaseki
NTT霞ヶ関

Yūrakuchō Int'l Arcade

Dōwa Bldg
同和ビル

Ginza No

Jiji Press
時事通信社

Fukoku Mutual
Life Insurance
富国生命

Dai-Ichi Kangyō
Bank (H.O.)
第一勧銀(本店)

不二家
Fujiya

GINZA DORI
銀座通り

Recruit
リクルート

Uchisaiwaichō (1)
内幸町

Tokyo Electric
Power (H.O.)
東京電力(本社)

SUKIYABASHI
数寄屋橋次路

New Ginza Bldg
ニュー銀座ビル

Dentsū
電通

UCHISAIWAICHO
内幸町

Saiwai Bldg
幸ビル

Hibiya Dai Bldg
日比谷ダイビル

YAMANOTE LINE
山手線

Nitta Bldg
新田ビル

Shiseido (H
資生堂

Shinhibiya Bldg
新日比谷ビル

Tokyo Mutual
Life Insurance
東京生命

NTT

Aviation Bldg
(Kōkū Kaikan)
航空会館

Tōshin Bldg
東新ビル

Shimbashi Dai-Ichi Hotel
新橋第一ホテル

TOKAIDO LINE
東海道本線

ⓗGinza Nikkō Hotel
銀座日航ホテル

Shiz
資生

Kyōei Fire & Marine
Insurance 共栄火災海上
Asahi Bank
あさひ銀行

Shimbashi
(1)
新橋1丁目

Shizuoka
Newspaper & Broadcasting
静岡新聞,静岡放送

Recruit
リクルート

Shise
資生

SOTOBORIDORI

Fuji Bank
富士銀行

Dobashi Ramp
土橋ランプ

Mitsui Urban Hotel
三井アーバンホテル

ⓗGinza Kokusai
銀座国際ビル

SHUTO EXPWY
首都高速

akucho-Bldg
町ビル

Tokyo Kōtsū Kaikan
東京交通会館

Nishi-Ginza Ramp
西銀座ランプ

SHINKANSEN 新幹線

JRAKUCHO STATION

(2)

Yūraku Cinema
有楽シネマ

Nishi-Ginza Bldg
西銀座ビル

GINZA-ITCHOME

Namikiza
並木座

Fuji Bank
富士銀行

Nichigeki Tōhō 日劇東宝 (9Fl)
Piccadilly ピカデリー (9Fl)
Asahi Hall 朝日ホール (11Fl)
Nihon Theater 日本劇場 (11Fl)

Ginza(2)
銀座二丁目

Printemps Ginza
Dept Store
プランタン銀座

Playguide Bldg
プレイガイドビル

Ginza Melsa
銀座メルサ

Yūrakuchō Mullion
有楽町マリオン

nkyu Dept Store
阪急デパート

Seibu Dept Store
西武デパート

Tōei Kaikan (hall)
東映会館

Tokyo Central Mus. of Art
東京セントラル美術館

Daiwa Bank
大和銀行

Kanebō Signas
カネボウシグナス

Itōya Stationery
伊東屋

Nishiginza Dept Store

GINZA 銀座

Ginza Ch.
銀座教会

Ginza AS Bldg
銀座ASビル

Matsuya
Dept Store
松屋デパート

Sukyabashi
Hankyū Dept Store
数寄屋橋阪急デパート

Fuji Bank
富士銀行

GINZA LINE

Ginza(3)
銀座3丁目

Sony Bldg
ソニービル

Kyobunkan Bldg
教文館ビル

Ginza Bunka 銀座文化

日動火災海上

Nichidō Fire &
Marine Insurance

Sukiya Camera
スキヤカメラ

Mikimoto
ミキモト Pearl

Wakō
和光

Sanwa Bank
三和銀行

Ginza Miyukikan Theater
銀座みゆき劇場

MIYUKI DORI みゆき通り

Mitsukoshi
Dept Store
三越デパート

Ōji Paper
王子製紙

Ginza(4)
銀座4丁目

Scn'ai
三愛

Asahi Bldg
朝日ビル

New Melsa
ニューメルサ

日本交通公社
JTB

Ginza Core
銀座コア

Japanese
Sake Center
日本酒センター

Meiyū Int'l Bldg
明裕国際会館

Komatsu Annex
小松アネックス

Dai-Ichi Kangyō Bank
第一勧銀

Ginza(5)
銀座5丁目

Tokyo Sōwa Bank
東京相和銀行

Kōjunsha Bldg
交詢社ビル

Ginza Komatsu
銀座小松

松坂屋デパート
Matsuzakaya
Dept Store

Kabuki-za
(theater)
歌舞伎座

SUZURAN DORI すずらん通り

Tōkai Bank
東海銀行

Sapporo Beer Hall
サッポロビヤホール

Ginza(6)
銀座6丁目

Honshu Paper Bldg
本州製紙ビル

HIGASHI

tō Pavilion
パビリオン

Tōshiba Ginza
東芝銀座

HIGASHI-GINZA

Sapporo Breweries
サッポロビール

Tokyo Spa (onsen)
東京温泉

Nichidō Fire &
Marine Insurance
日動火災海上

nza
Gas Hall
ガスホール

Yamaha Hall
ヤマハホール

銀座東武ホテル
Ginza Tōbu Hotel

Nankai Tokyo Bldg
南海東京ビル

Mitsubishi Bank
三菱銀行

Ginza(7)
銀座7丁目

Nagasaki Center Bldg
長崎センタービル

TOEI ASAKUSA LINE 都営浅草線

Ginza Tōkyū Hotel
銀座東急ホテル

DORI

Dai-ichi Tekkō Bldg 第一鉄鋼ビル

Sakura Bank さくら銀行

(H)Ryūmeikan 竜名館

Sumitomo Marine & Fire Insurance 住友海上

Fukuoka City Bank 福岡シティ銀行

日本興業銀行 Industrial Bank of Japan

Hokkaidō Takushoku Bank 北海道拓銀

柳屋ビル Yanagiya Bldg

Nihombas 日本橋

Tōkyū 東急テ

Dai-ni Tekkō Bldg 第二鉄鋼ビル

Tōyō Trust 東洋信託

TOKYO STATION

(H)Kokusai Kankō Kaikan 国際観光会館

Yaesu North Entrance 八重洲北口

Yaesu (1) 八重洲1丁目

Bank of Osaka 大阪銀行

Gunma Bank 群馬銀行

Nippon Fire & Marine Insurance Bldg 日本火災ビル

Sanwa Bank 三和銀行

住友 Sumitome

Bank

Fuji Bank 富士銀行

Nihombashi Plaza Bldg 日本橋プラザビル

Nihombashi (2) 日本橋2丁目

Daimaru Dept Store 大丸デパート

Yaesuguchi Kaikan (hall) 八重洲口会館

Maruzen 丸善

Dai-Ichi Kangyō Bank 第一勧銀

Tokyo Sōwa Bank 東京相和銀行

Tokyo Tatemono Bldg 東京建物ビル

Nippon Trust (H.O.) 日本信託(本社)

Takashimaya Dept Store 高島屋デパート

〒日本橋通局 Taiyo Mutual Nihombashidōri P.O. Life Insurance 太陽生命

Yanmer Bldg ヤンマービル

Yaesu (2) 八重洲2丁目

Yaesu Bldg 八重洲ビル

Ōsaka Bldg 大阪ビル

Jōto E. Sch. 城東小

Nihombashi (3) 日本橋3丁目

東京銀行 Bank of Tokyo Dōwa Bldg 同和ビル

Sumitomo Trust (H.O.) 住友信託(本部)

Asahi Bank あさひ銀行

Bridgestone Mus. of Art ブリヂストン美術館

Higashi Nippon Bank 東日本銀行（本店）

Yaesu Book Center 八重洲ブックセンター

Shin Yaesu Bldg 新八重洲ビル

Chuo Trust (H.O.) 中央信託(本店)

Kyōbashi (1) 京橋1丁目

Chiba Kogyo Bank 千葉興業銀行

Dai-Ich Bank 第一勧

Ajinomoto (H.O.) 味の素(本社)

Mitsubishi Ba 三菱銀

Takar

Chiyoda Bldg 千代田ビル

Nichimen ニチメン

Uchida Yōkō 内田洋行

Meijiya Store 明治屋

Ōita Bank 大分銀行

Chuokoron-sha 中央公論社

Ajinomoto Bldg 味の素ビル

Meiji Seika 明治製菓

Yamagataya Laver Shop 山形屋のり店

(No.1)

Kyōbashi Dai-ichi Seimei Bldg 京橋第一生命ビル

Nurihiko Bldg ぬ利彦ビル

(No.2)

Shimizu Corp. 清水建設

Kyōbashi (2) 京橋2丁目

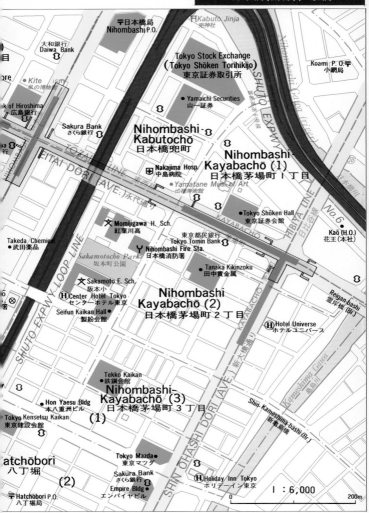

〒日本橋局
Nihombashi P.O.

H Kabuto Jinja
兜神社

目

大和銀行
Daiwa Bank

Koami P.O. 〒
小網局

Tokyo Stock Exchange
(Tokyo Shōken Torihikijo)
東京証券取引所

ore ● Kite
凧の博物館

● Yamaichi Securities
山一証券

k of Hiroshima
広島銀行

Sakura Bank
さくら銀行

Nihombashi-
Kabutocho
日本橋兜町

Nihombashi
Kayabachō (1)
日本橋茅場町 1 丁目

行

EITAI DORI AVE. 永代通り

TOSAN LINE

● Nakajima Hosp.
中島病院

Yamatane Mus. of Art
山種美術館

a 8

HIBIYA LINE

No.6

● Tokyo Shōken Hall
東京証券会館

KAYABACHO

Kaō (H.O.)
花王(本社)

文 Momijigawa H. Sch.
紅葉川高

Takeda Chemical
● 武田薬品

東京都民銀行
Tokyo Tomin Bank 8
日本橋消防署

Sakamotocho Park
坂本町公園

Y Nihombashi Fire Sta.

Tanaka Kikinzoku
田中貴金属

SHUTO EXPWY. LOOP LINE

文 Sakamoto E. Sch.
阪本小
H Center Hotel Tokyo
センターホテル東京

Nihombashi
Kayabachō (2)
日本橋茅場町 2 丁目

Reigan-bashi
霊岸橋(Br.)

8

Seifun Kaikan Hall ●
製粉会館

新大橋通り SHIN OHASHI DORI

H Hotel Universe
ホテルユニバース

客

⊗

Tekko Kaikan
● 鉄鋼会館

Nihombashi-
Kayabachō (3)
日本橋茅場町 3 丁目

Shin Kameshima-bashi (Br.)
新亀島橋

ろ

● Hon Yaesu Bldg
本八重洲ビル

(1)

Kameshima Gawa
亀島川

● Tokyo Kensetsu Kaikan
東京建設会館

atchōbori
八丁堀

Tokyo Mazda ●
東京マツダ

(2)

Sakura Bank
さくら銀行 8
Empire Bldg
エンパイヤビル

H Holiday Inn Tokyo
ホリデーイン東京

1 : 6,000

〒Hatchōbori P.O.
八丁堀局

0   200m

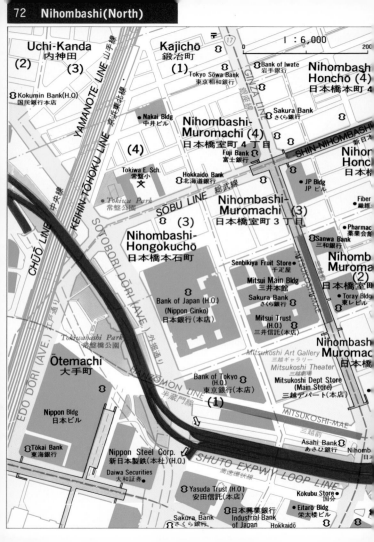

Uchi-Kanda
内神田
(2)　　(3)

Kajichō
鍛冶町
(1)

〒

⑰

1:6,000
0 _____ 200

🏦 Bank of Iwate
岩手銀行

Nihombash
Honchō (4)
日本橋本町4

🏦 Tokyo Sōwa Bank
東京相和銀行

🏦 Kokumin Bank (H.O)
国民銀行本店

GINZA LINE

• Nakai Bldg
中井ビル

Nihombashi-
Muromachi (4)
日本橋室町4丁目

🏦 Sakura Bank
さくら銀行

SHIN-NIHOMBASH

Nihor
Honc
日本

YAMANOTE LINE

KEIHIN-TOHOKU LINE

京浜東北線

(4)

Tokiwa E. Sch.
常盤小

🏫

Fuji Bank 🏦
富士銀行

🏦 Hokkaido Bank
北海道銀行

総武線

• JP Bldg
JP ビル

Fiber
繊維

CHŪŌ LINE
中央線

• Tokiwa Park
常盤公園

SOBU LINE

(3)

Nihombashi-
Muromachi (3)
日本橋室町3丁目

🏦 Sanwa Bank
三和銀行

• Pharmac
薬業会館

Nihomb
Muroma
(2)
日本橋室町

SONOBORI-DŌRI AVE.

Nihombashi-
Hongokuchō
日本橋本石町

Senbikiya Fruit Store •
千疋屋

Mitsui Main Bldg
三井本館

Sakura Bank 🏦
さくら銀行

Mitsui Trust
(H.O.) 🏦
三井信託(本店)

• Toray Bldg
東レビル

Bank of Japan (H.O.)
(Nippon Ginko)
日本銀行(本店)

🏦

Mitsukoshi Art Gallery
三越ギャラリー

Nihombash
Muromac
日本橋

Tokiwahashi Park
常盤橋公園

Otemachi
大手町

EDO DŌRI (AVE.) 江戸通り

HANZOMON LINE
半蔵門線

外堀通り

Bank of Tokyo
(H.O.)
東京銀行(本店)

🏦

Mitsukoshi Theater
三越劇場

Mitsukoshi Dept Store
(Main Store)
三越デパート(本店)

(1)

MITSUKOSHI-MAE

三越前

Nippon Bldg
日本ビル

🏦

🏦 Tōkai Bank
東海銀行

Nippon Steel Corp.
新日本製鉄(本社)(H.O.)

Daiwa Securities
大和証券 •

Asahi Bank 🏦
あさひ銀行

Nihomb
日本

SHUTO EXPWY LOOP LINE
高速道路環状線

Yasuda Trust (H.O.)
安田信託(本店)

🏦 日本興業銀行
Industrial Bank
of Japan

Kokubu Store
国分

• Eitaro Bldg
栄太楼ビル

Sakura Bank
さくら銀行

🏦

Hokkaidō

Shiga Bank
滋賀銀行

Nihombashi-Odenmachō
日本橋大伝馬町

Mitsubishi Bank
三菱銀行

Sumitomo Bank
住友銀行

Michinoku Bank
みちのく銀行

Tokyo Credit Assoc.
東京信金

EDO DORI AVE. 江戸通り

Nihombashi-Horidomebashi P.O
日本橋堀留橋局

Sakura Bank
さくら銀行

SHUTO EXPWY No.

Takarada Ebisu Jinja
宝田恵比寿神社

Nihombashi Tax Office
日本橋税務署

Sanwa Bank
三和銀行

Shizuoka Bank
静岡銀行

Business Hotel Villa
ビジネスホテルヴィラ

ランプ
p Ramp
ー
）

Shin Horidome
Kyōdo Bldg
新堀留共同ビル

Dai-Ichi Kangyō Bank
第一勧銀

丁 3丁目

Nihombashi Honchō Bldg
日本橋ホンチョービル

**Nihombashi-
Horidomechō**
日本橋堀留町

(2)
Daiwa Bank
大和銀行

**Nihombashi
Honchō (2)**
日本橋本町 2丁目

Ishikawa Bank
石川銀行

(1)
Sakura Bank
さくら銀行

Nihombashi
Kobunachō P.O
日本橋小舟町局

Nihombashi Health Center
日本橋保健所

Nippon Trust
日本信託

Honcho Ramp
本町ランプ

目

**Nihombashi-
Kobunachō**
日本橋小舟町

Horidome Children's Park
堀留児童公園

(3)

Tokyo City Hotel
東京シティホテル

**Nihombashi-
Honchō (1)**
日本橋本町 1丁目

**Nihombashi-
Ningyōchō**
日本橋人形町

丁目

8

Laver Shop
店

Fuji Bank Mus.
富士銀行資料館

Fuji Bank
富士
銀行

TOEI ASAKUSA LINE
都営浅草線

(1)

ga Bank
銀行

Edobashi Ramp
江戸橋ランプ

Edobashi Ramp
江戸橋ランプ

Tōyōbō Bldg
東洋紡ビル

Edobashi I.C.
江戸橋インター

Edobashi J.C.
江戸橋J.C.

Nihombashi-Koamichō
日本橋小網町

Nissin Flour Milling (H.O.)
日清製粉（本社）

Nomura Securities
野村証券

Edo-bashi (Br.)
江戸橋
Mitsubishi Warehouse &
Transportation Trunk Room
三菱倉庫トランクルーム

ank
銀

Nihombashi P.O.
日本橋局

Kabuto Jinja
兜神社

✕ Nihon Univ. (Econ.)
日本大(経済)
(2)

Meiji H.Sch.
明治高
YMCA

Sanraku Hosp.
三楽病院

Hamada Hosp.
浜田病院

Tokyo Met. Cancer
Detection Center
東京都がん検診センター

Ochanomi
御茶の水

STA
御茶の

Kanda Jogakuen (Sch.)
神田女学園
(1)

Bunka Gakuin (Sch.)
文化学院
(2)

杏雲堂病
Kyōundō He

Sarugakuchō
猿楽町

(1)

Kanda-Surugadai
神田駿河台

✕ Meiji Univ.
明治大

Nichidai Ho
日大病院

HAKUSAN DŌRI AVE.
白山通り

(1)

Kitajinbōchō P.O.
北神保町局

Hilltop Hotel
山の上ホテル

YWCA
(Dental)
(歯)

Nihon Un
日本大
(Sci.&E
(理工)

(2)

Kanda-Jimbōchō
神田神保町
(1)

Meiji Univ.
明治大

錦華小
Kinka E.Sch.

Meiji Univ.
Administrative Bldg
明治大学(本部)

(1)

Ochanomizu Square
お茶の水スクエア

Casals Hall
カザルスホール

NTT

Mitsui Mari
Insurance (N
三井海上(

KANDA BOOKSHOPS AREA 神田書店街

JIMBŌCHŌ 神保町

靖国通り

TOEI SHINJUKU LINE
都営新宿線

Iwanami Hall
岩波ホール

Tuttle Books
タトル

Sanseidō
三省堂

Ogawamachi P.O.
小川町局

(3)

SAKURA DŌRI
さくら通り

JIMBŌCHŌ

SUZURAN DŌRI
すずらん通り

Ogawa E.Sch.
小川小

Kanda-Ogawa
神田小

Taiheiyo Bank
太平洋銀行

SPORTING GOODS

スポーツ用品店街
都営新宿線

AREA

Hotel Hitotsubashi
ホテルヒトツバシ

CHIYODA-KU
千代田区

Mizuno
美津濃

Hitotsubashi Hall
一橋ホール

Hitotsubashi Jr.H.Sch
一橋中

Shogakukan
小学館

Sanwa
三和銀

Hitotsubashi
一ツ橋

(2)

Kyōritsu Joshigakuen (Sch.)
共立女子学園

Kyōritsu Kōdō (Hall)
共立講堂

Gakushi Kaikan
学士会館

Hakuhōdō
博報堂

Tokyo Electrical Engg Coll.
東京電機大

Kanda Health Center
神田保健所

Hitotsubashi Kōdō
一ツ橋講堂

Kanda Tax Office
神田税務署

(3)

Seisoku Gakuen
正則学園

Kanda Police Sta.
神田署

(1)

Sumitomo Corp.
住友商事
(1)

NTT

Josui Kaikan
如水会館

Kinjo Gakuen
錦城学園

Shin Tokyo Hotel
新東京ホテル

(2)

Tenri Galle
天理ギャラ

Tenri Bldg
天理ビル

EXPWY LOOP LINE

Kanda-Nishikichō
神田錦町

Palace Side Bldg
パレスサイドビル

Mainichi Newspapers
毎日新聞

Hitotsubashi Ramp
一ツ橋ランプ

Tokyo Gas
東京ガス

Yushima Seidō
湯島聖堂

bashi
聖橋

IZU

(4)

Nikorai
Cathedral
ニコライ
聖堂

ban

CHIYODA LINE

Kanda-gawa
神田川

AKIHABARA
ELECTRICAL GOODS AREA
秋葉原電気器具街

Nippon Express
(Nittsu) Bldg
日通ビル

(3)

Yamagiwa
ヤマギワ

Ishimaru Denki
石丸電気

Hirose Radio
& Electric
広瀬無線

Akihabara Dept Store
秋葉原デパート

GINZA LINE

AKIHABARA STATION

Hitachi (H.Q.)
日立(本社)

(2)

SŌBU LINE

Shōhei-bashi (Br.)
昌平橋

総武線

Laox
ラオックス

17

Soto-
Kanda

外神田
1丁目

秋葉原駅

Hotel Juraku
ホテル聚楽

Nagura Hosp.
名倉病院

Kanda Fire Sta.
神田消防署

神田局
Kanda P.O.

Manseibashi Police Sta.
万世橋署

Mansei-bashi (Br.)
万世橋

Awaji E. Sch.
淡路小

Hotel New Kanda
ホテルニュー神田

Mansei
万世

Tokyo Green Hotel Awajichō
東京グリーンホテル淡路町

Transportation
Musm.
交通博物館

SHIN-OCHANOMIZU

Kanda-Awajichō
神田淡路町

Dōwa Hosp.
同和病院

Kanda-Sudacho
神田須田町

Zendentsū
Hall
全電通ホール

Sōhyō Kaikan
総評会館

(1)

YASUKUNI DŌRI

靖国通り

CHŪŌ LINE

DŌRI (AVE.)

ni

(1)

OGAWAMACHI (AVE.)

AWAJICHŌ DŌRI

Kanda-Sudachō (1)
神田須田町1丁目

中央線

Tōkai Bank
東海銀行

小川町

淡路町

Kanda-
Tachō
神田多町

Kanda
Kajichō
(3)

Kanda-
Mitoshiro-
chō
(1)

神田
美土代町

YMCA

Kanda-
Tsukasamachi
神田司町

SOTOBORI DŌRI

New Central Hotel
ニューセントラルホテル

Kandaekimae P.O.
神田駅前局

神田
鍛治町
(3)

KEIHIN-TŌHOKU LINE

Ohbayashi Corp.
大林組

Kanda E. Sch.
神田小

NTT Kanda
NTT神田

Grand Central Hotel
グランドセントラル
ホテル

Kajichō
(2)

鍛治町2丁目

KANDA STATION

Tokyo Royal Plaza
東京ロイヤルプラザ

Central Hotel
セントラルホテル

Uchi-Kanda
(3)

内神田

Imagawa Jr.H.Sch
今川中

Uchi-Kanda
(1)

内神田1丁目

Kanda Inst. of
Foreign Languages
神田外語学院

内神田
3丁目

1 : 8,000

0   200m

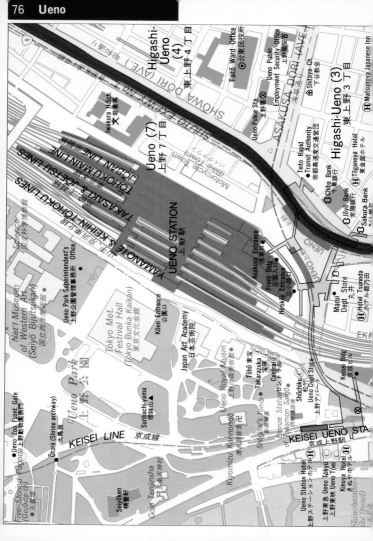

1 : 6,000

0 ─── 200m

Senzoku (6)
浅草 6 丁目

Hanakawado (2)
花川戸 2 丁目

Asahi Shinkin Bank
朝日信用金庫

Taitō Ward Hall
台東区民会館

Tokyo Trade Center
(Taitō Hall)
都産業貿易センター

Hanakawado Park
花川戸公園

Asakusa E.Sch.

女浅草

Asakusa Jinja (Shr.)
浅草神社

Niten-mon
二天門

Asakusa Kannondō
浅草観音堂

Asakusa (3)
浅草 3 丁目

Kannari Gorogorō Kaikan
冠555会館

Sensō-ji Hosp.
浅草寺病院

Awashima-dō
あわしま堂

Yakushi-dō
薬師堂

六ぢぞ-mon
六区門

Sensō-ji (temple)
浅草寺

Five-Storied Pagoda
五重塔

Gojino-tō

Sukeroku

Asakusa Park
浅草公園

Fuji Bank
第1勧銀

Asakusa (2)
浅草 2 丁目

Lions Mansion
ライオンズマンション

Hanayashiki
Amusement Park
花やしき遊園地

Mokuba-kan
木馬館

浅草歴史資料館 浅草屋伝承館

Denbōin Garden
伝法院庭園

Dai-ichi Kangyō Bank
第一勧銀

Taitō Traditional
Crafts Musm
台東区伝統工芸美術館

SENZOKU DORI
千束通り

HISAGO DORI

Asakusa Tōei
浅草東映

Asakusa Shingekijō
浅草新劇場

WINS Asakusa
ウインズ浅草

Asakusa Tōhō
浅草東宝

Nishi-Sando
西参道

Asakusa Bowl
浅草ボウル

KOTOTOI DORI (AVE.)

Asakusa Chūei
浅草中央

Rock-za Kaikan
ロック座会館

Asakusa Engei Hall
浅草演芸ホール

KOKUSAI DORI (AVE.)
国際通り

Senzoku (1)
千束 1 丁目

Banryū-ji
万隆寺

TengaKein
天嶽院

Asakusa View Hotel
浅草ビューホテル

Nichirinji
十輪寺

Asakusa Ch.
浅草教会

Nishi-Asakusa (3)
西浅草 3 丁目

Asakusa
Handicrafts Musm
(Asakusa Kōgei-kan)
浅草工芸館

浅草 タワー
東京タワー

西浅草 2丁目
(2)

Sakura Bank さくら銀行
交番

Drum-Mush 太鼓館

Asakusa Shōchiku 浅草松竹

卍

卍 卍 卍 卍

卍

Nishi-Asakusa 西浅草 (1)

卍

Asakusa P.O. 〒浅草局

卍 東本願寺事務所

卍 田原町

卍 Kinryū-ji

TAWARAMACHI 田原町

GINZA LINE 銀座線

(2)

(1)

Asakusa Public Hall 浅草公会堂

(H)三河屋別館 Ryōkan Mikawaya Bekkan

SHIN NAKAMISE DŌRI 新仲見世通り

KANNON DŌRI 観音通り

ORANGE DŌRI 浅草 オレンジ通り

新仲見世通り

Asakusa (1) 浅草 一丁目

CHINYOKO DŌRI ちんや横丁

Kaminarimon 雷門通り

Mitsubishi Bank 三菱銀行

Kaminarimon (1) 雷門 一丁目

Tōkai Bank 東海銀行

Tokyo Sōwa Bank 東京相和

Fuji Bank 富士銀行

SUSHIYA DŌRI すしや通り

ASAKUSA DŌRI (AVE.) 浅草通り

Religious Goods Town 仏壇街

Tawara E-Sch. 大田原小

Metropolitan Tax Office 台東都税事務所

⊗

NTT Asakusa NTT浅草

Tokyo Toyota 東京トヨタ

Y

Kotobuki 寿 (4)

(3)

卍 Kurofune Jinja 黒船神社

卍 Kinryū-ji

NAKAMISE DŌRI 仲見世通り

Kaminarimon 雷門

Sumitomo Bank 住友銀行

Kaminarimon (2) 雷門 二丁目

雷門 2丁目

Kaminarimon Skymansion 雷門スカイマンション

KANNON DŌRI

Shinsui Park 隅田公園

Waterbus Station 水上バスのりば

TOBU ASAKUSA STATION 東武浅草駅

TOBU ASAKUSA Dept Store 東武浅草デパート

Matsuya Dept Store 松屋デパート

6

Kamiya Bar 神谷バー

Kaminarimon 雷門

Kaminarimon P.O. 雷門局

(H)

Asakusa Tourist Information Center 浅草文化観光センター

TOEI ASAKUSA LINE 都営浅草線

EDO DŌRI (AVE.) 江戸通り

Mugitoro むぎとろ

Komagata-dō 駒形堂

(2)

Bank of Tokyo 東京銀行

Sanwa Bank 三和銀行

Komagata (1) 駒形 (1)

World Bags Museum 世界のカバン館

Sumida Gawa (River) 隅田川

Azuma-bashi (Br.) 吾妻橋

(1) Azuma-bashi 吾妻橋

Komagata-bashi (Br.) 駒形橋

Komagata 駒形

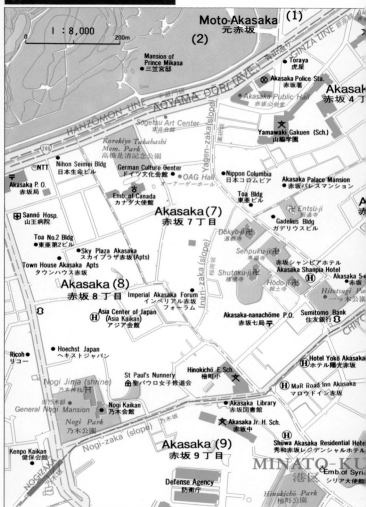

Moto-Akasaka **(1)**
元赤坂

(2)

I : 8,000

0   200m

Mansion of
Prince Mikasa
三笠宮邸

• Toraya
虎屋

⊗ Akasaka Police Sta.
赤坂署

Akasaka Public Hall
赤坂公会堂

文 Yamawaki Gakuen (Sch.)
山脇学園

Akasaka
赤坂4丁

HANZOMON LINE   AOYAMA DORI (AVE.)

GINZA LINE

Sogetsu Art Center
草月会館

Korekiyo Takahashi
Mem. Park
高橋是清記念公園

248

Nihon Seimei Bldg
日本生命ビル

German Culture Center
ドイツ文化会館

• OAG Hall
オーアーゲーホール

• Nippon Columbia
日本コロムビア

Akasaka Palace Mansion
• 赤坂パレスマンション

NTT

Akasaka P. O.
赤坂局

Emb. of Canada
カナダ大使館

Toa Bldg
東亜ビル

Akasaka (7)
赤坂7丁目

Entsū-ji 卍
円通寺

Gadelius Bldg
ガデリウスビル

A
赤

✚ Sannō Hosp.
山王病院

Dōkyō-ji 卍
道教寺

Senpuku-ji 卍
専福寺

赤坂シャンピアホテル
Akasaka Shanpia Hotel

• Toa No.2 Bldg
東亜第2ビル

• Sky Plaza Akasaka
スカイプラザ赤坂 (Apts)

Shutoku-ji 卍
種徳寺

Hōdo-ji 卍
宝土寺 H

Akasaka 5
赤坂

Town House Akasaka Apts
タウンハウス赤坂

Hitotsugi Pa
一ツ木

Akasaka (8)
赤坂8丁目

Imperial Akasaka Forum
インペリアル赤坂
フォーラム

Akasaka-nanachōme P.O.
赤坂七局 〒

Sumitomo Bank
住友銀行 ⑧

⑧

Ⓗ Asia Center of Japan (Asia Kaikan)
アジア会館

CHIY

Ricoh •
リコー

• Hoechst Japan
ヘキストジャパン

St Paul's Nunnery
聖パウロ女子修道会

Hinokichō E. Sch.
檜町小

文

Ⓗ Hotel Yokō Akasaka
ホテル陽光赤坂

Nogi Jinja (shrine)
乃木神社 卍

Nogi Kaikan
乃木会館

• Akasaka Library
赤坂図書館

Ⓗ MaR Road Inn Akasaka
マロウドイン赤坂

General Nogi Mansion

Nogi Park
乃木公園

文 Akasaka Jr. H. Sch.
赤坂中

Nogi-zaka (slope)

Akasaka (9)
赤坂9丁目

Ⓗ Shūwa Akasaka Residential Hote
秀和赤坂レジデンシャルホテル

NOGIZAKA

Kenpo Kaikan
健保会館

MINATO-KU
港区

• Emb. of Syri
シリア大使館

Defense Agency
防衛庁

Hinokichō Park
檜町公園

Yagen-zaka (slope)

Inari-zaka (slope)

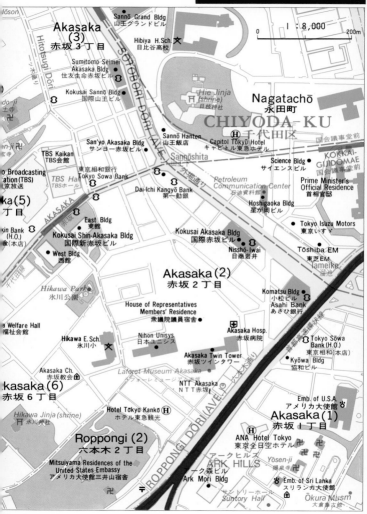

Iōson

Akasaka (3)
赤坂3丁目

Hitotsugi Dōri 一ツ木通り

do-ji
土寺

n-ji
寺

Sannō Grand Bldg
山王グランドビル

Hibiya H.Sch.
日比谷高校 文

Sumitomo Seimei
Akasaka Bldg
住友生命赤坂ビル

Kokusai Sannō Bldg
国際山王ビル

SOTOBORI-DŌRI 外堀通り

Hie Jinja
(shrine)
日枝神社 ⛩

Nagatachō
永田町

CHIYODA - KU
千代田区

国会議事堂前

0 1:8,000 200m

Sannō Hanten
山王飯店

San'yo Akasaka Bldg
サンヨー赤坂ビル

Capitol Tōkyū Hotel
キャピトル東急ホテル Ⓗ

Science Bldg
サイエンスビル

KOKKAI-
GIJIDŌMAE
国会議事堂前

TBS Kaikan
TBS会館

Sannōshita
山王下

o Broadcasting
ation (TBS)
京放送

Tōkyō Sowa Bank
東京相和銀行

SOTOBORI-DŌRI

Petroleum
Communication Center
石油資料館

Prime Minister's
Official Residence
首相官邸

TBS Hall
TBSホール

Dai-Ichi Kangyō Bank
第一勧銀

Hoshigaoka Bldg
星が岡ビル

ka (5)
丁目

AKASAKA 赤坂

East Bldg
東館

Kokusai Akasaka Bldg
国際赤坂ビル

Tokyo Isuzu Motors
東京いすゞ

in Bank
(H.O.)
金(本店)

Kokusai Shin-Akasaka Bldg
国際新赤坂ビル

Nissho-Iwai
日商岩井

Tōshiba EM
東芝EM.

West Bldg
西館

Akasaka (2)
赤坂2丁目

Tameike
溜池

Hikawa Park
氷川公園

House of Representatives
Members' Residence
衆議院議員宿舎

Komatsu Bldg
小松ビル

Asahi Bank
あさひ銀行

a Welfare Hall
福祉会館

Hikawa E.Sch.
氷川小 文

Nihon Unisys
日本ユニシス

Akasaka Hosp. ✚
赤坂病院

Tokyo Sōwa
Bank (H.O.)
東京相和(本店)

Kyōwa Bldg
協和ビル

kasaka (6)
赤坂6丁目

Akasaka Ch.
赤坂教会

Akasaka Twin Tower
赤坂ツインタワー

Laforet Museum Akasaka
ラフォーレミュージアム

NTT Akasaka
NTT赤坂

Emb. of U.S.A
アメリカ大使館 ♂

Hikawa Jinja (shrine)
氷川神社 ⛩

Hotel Tōkyū Kankō Ⓗ
ホテル東急観光

Akasaka (1)
赤坂1丁目

ANA Hotel Tokyo Ⓗ
東京全日空ホテル

Yōsen-ji
陽泉寺 卍

Roppongi (2)
六本木2丁目

ROPPONGI DŌRI (AVE.) 六本木通り

ARK HILLS
アークヒルズ

卍

Mitsuiyama Residences of the
United States Embassy
アメリカ大使館三井山宿舎

卍

Ark Mori Bldg
アーク森ビル

Emb. of Sri Lanka
スリランカ大使館 ♂

サントリーホール
Suntory Hall

Ōkura Musm
大倉集古館

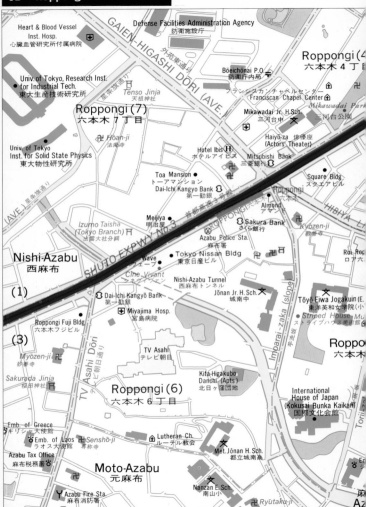

Heart & Blood Vessel
Inst. Hosp.
心臓血管研究所付属病院

Defense Facilities Administration Agency
防衛施設庁

GAIEN-HIGASHI DORI (AVE.)
外苑東通り

Roppongi (4
六本木 4 丁目

Bōeichōnai P.O.
防衛庁内局

Univ. of Tokyo, Research Inst.
for Industrial Tech.
東大生産技術研究所

フランシスカンチャペルセンター
Franciscan Chapel Center

Mikawadai Park

Tenso Jinja
天祖神社

Roppongi (7)
六本木 (7) 丁目

Mikawadai Jr. H.Sch.
三河台中

三河台公園

Hōan-ji
法願寺

Haiyū-za 俳優座
(Actors' Theater)

Univ. of Tokyo
Inst. for Solid State Physics
東大物性研究所

Hotel Ibis Ⓗ
ホテルアイビス

Mitsubishi Bank
三菱銀行

Square Bldg
スクエアビル

Toa Mansion ●
トーアマンション
Dai-Ichi Kangyo Bank
第一勧銀

Roppongi
六本木

Almond
アマンド

HIBIYA

Izumo Taisha
(Tokyo Branch)
出雲大社分祠

Meijiya ●
明治屋

Sakura Bank
さくら銀行

Kyōzen-ji
鏡専寺

Nishi-Azabu
西麻布

Azabu Police Sta.
麻布署

SHUTO EXPWY NO. 3

Wave
ウェーブ

Tokyo Nissan Bldg
東京日産ビル

Roi Rop
ロア六

(1)

Cine Vivant
シネヴィヴァン

Nishi-Azabu Tunnel
西麻布トンネル

Jōnan Jr. H.Sch.
城南中

Tōyō Eiwa Jogakuin (E.
東洋英和女学院(小

Dai-Ichi Kangyō Bank
第一勧銀

Imparai-zaka (Slope
芋洗坂

Striped House Mu
ストライプハウス美術館

(3)

Roppongi Fuji Bldg
六本木フジビル

Miyajima Hosp.
宮島病院

Myōzen-ji
妙善寺

TV Asahi
テレビ朝日

Roppo
六本木

Sakurada Jinja
桜田神社

TV Asahi Dōri
テレビ朝日通り

Roppongi (6)
六本木 6 丁目

Kita-Higakubo
Danchi (Apts)
北ヶ窪団地

International
House of Japan
(Kokusai Bunka Kaikan)
国際文化会館

Tori

Emb. of Greece
ギリシャ大使館

Emb. of Laos
ラオス大使館

Senshō-ji
専称寺

Lutheran Ch.
ルーテル教会

Met. Jōnan H. Sch.
都立城南高

Azabu Tax Office
麻布税務署

Moto-Azabu
元麻布

Nanzan E. Sch.
南山小

Az

Azabu Fire Sta.
麻布消防署

Ryūtaku-ji
龍沢寺

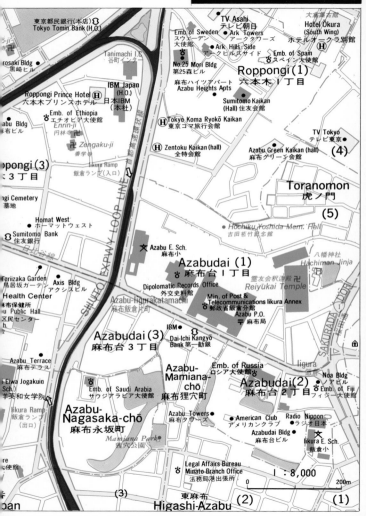

東京都民銀行(本店)
Tokyo Tomin Bank (H.O.)

rosaki Bldg
黒崎ビル

TV Asahi
テレビ朝日

Emb. of Sweden
スウェーデン
大使館

Ark Towers
アークタワーズ

Hotel Ōkura
(South Wing)
ホテルオークラ別館

Ark Hills Side
アークヒルズサイド

Tanimachi I.C.
谷町インター

No.25 Mori Bldg
第25森ビル

Emb. of Spain
スペイン大使館

IBM Japan
(H.O.)
日本IBM
(本社)

Roppongi (1)
六本木 1 丁目

Roppongi Prince Hotel
六本木プリンスホテル

麻布ハイツアパート
Azabu Heights Apts

布ビル
Bldg

Emb. of Ethiopia
エチオピア大使館

Enrin-ji
円林寺卍

Sumitomo Kaikan 住友会館
住友会館

卍 Zengaku-ji
善学寺

Tokyo Koma Ryokō Kaikan
東京コマ旅行会館

TV Tokyo
テレビ東京

oppongi (3)
: 3丁目

Iikura Ramp
飯倉ランプ(入口)

Zentoku Kaikan (hall)
全特会館

Azabu Green Kaikan (hall)
麻布グリーン会館 (4)

ngi Cemetery
墓地

Toranomon
虎ノ門
(5)

Homat West
ホーマットウェスト

Hochiku Yoshida Mem. Hall
吉田筺竹記念館

Sumitomo Bank
住友銀行

文 Azabu E. Sch.
麻布小

八幡神社
Hachiman Jinja

oriizaka Garden
鳥居坂ガーデン

Axis Bldg
アクシスビル

Azabudai (1)
麻布台 1 丁目

Reiyūkai Temple
霊友会釈迦殿 卍

布保健所
Health Center

Dipolomatic Records Office
外交史料館

Min. of Post &
Telecommunications Iikura Annex
郵政省飯倉分庁

u Public Hall
区民センター

Azabu-Iigurakatamachi
麻布飯倉片町

Azabu P.O.
麻布局

IBM●

Azabudai (3)
麻布台 3 丁目

Dai-Ichi Kangyō
Bank 第一勧銀

Azabu Terrace
麻布テラス

Noa Bldg
ノアビル

Eiwa Jogakuin
Sch.)
英和女学院

Azabu-
Mamiana-
chō
麻布狸穴町

Emb. of Russia
ロシア大使館

Iigura
飯倉

Azabudai (2)
麻布台 2 丁目

Emb. of Fiji
フィジー大使館

iikura Ramp
飯倉ランプ
(出口)

Emb. of Saudi Arabia
サウジアラビア大使館

Azabu-
Nagasaka-chō
麻布永坂町

Azabu Towers●
麻布タワーズ

American Club
アメリカンクラブ

Radio Nippon
ラジオ日本

Azabudai Bldg
麻布台ビル

Iikura E. Sch.
飯倉小

Mamiana Park
狸穴公園

Legal Affairs Bureau
Minato Branch Office
法務局港出張所

1 : 8,000

0   200m

pan

(3)

東麻布
(2)

Higashi-Azabu
(1)

1 : 6,000

0   200m

◉ Shibuya Ward Office
渋谷区役所

Shibuya Health Center
渋谷保健所

Shibuya Homes
渋谷ホームズ

Ōmukai E. Sch.
大向小

KŌEN DŌRI (AVE.)

Tobacco & Salt M

たばこと塩の博物館

Jinnan
神南

Tōbu Hotel
東武ホテル

Kyōdō Bldg
共同ビル

Parco Part II
パルコパート 2

Jinnan Bldg
神南ビル

Workers' Welfare
勤労福祉セ

Shibuya Video Studio
渋谷ビデオスタジオ

Tōkyū Hands
東急ハンズ

Shibuya Parco Store
渋谷パルコ

Parco Part III
パルコパート 3

Parco Theater
パルコ劇場

Marui
Main
丸井本

Yamate Ch.
山手教会

Official Residence,
Governor of Tokyo
東京都知事公館

Tōkyū
Bunkamura
東急文化村

Udagawachō
宇田川町

Seibu Dept Store
西武デパート(シート
(SEED Bldg)

Joypack Bldg
ジョイパックビル

Quattro by Parco

Seibu Dept Store
西武デパート(Loft Bldg)
西武デパートロフト館

Palace-za
パレス座

(B Bldg)
B 館

Orchard Hall (3F)
オーチャードホール

Tōkyū Dept Store
(main store)
東急デパート(本店)

Tokyo Tomin Bank
東京都民銀行

ONE-OH-NINE 30S

西武デパ

Seibu Dept S
(A Bldg)
A 館

BUNKAMURA DŌRI (AVE.)
文化村通り

Sakura Bank
さくら銀行

Manyō Kaikan
万葉会館

Shibuya Takarazuka
渋谷宝塚

Shōtō P.O.
松濤局

Center-gai
センター街

Dai-Ichi Kangyō Bank
第一勧銀

Tōkai Bank
東海銀行

Dōgenzaka (2)
道玄坂 2 丁目

109 Fashion
Community
109 ファッションコ

The Prime
ザ・プライム

Dōgenzaka Center Bldg
道玄坂センタービル

Ekimae Bldg
駅前ビル

SHIB

Daiwa Bank
大和銀行

Interior Imon
インテリア井門

Shibutō Cinetower
渋東シネタワー

Battle of Dog Ha
ハチ

Tōkyū
Sto
東急東横店

Yachiyo Bank
八千代銀行

SHIBUYA STA.
渋谷駅

Maruyamachō
円山町

Noa Dōgenzaka
ノア道玄坂

Kita Nippon Bank
北日本銀行

Shin Taiso Bldg
新大宗ビル

Ekimae Kaikan
駅前会館

三菱ビル
Mitsubishi Bldg

Tōkyū Plaza
東急プラザ

Tram Depot
車庫

井の頭線
INOKASHIRA LINE

Dōgenzaka P.O.
道玄坂局

Dōgenzaka (1)
道玄坂 1 丁目

SHUTO EXPWY No.3

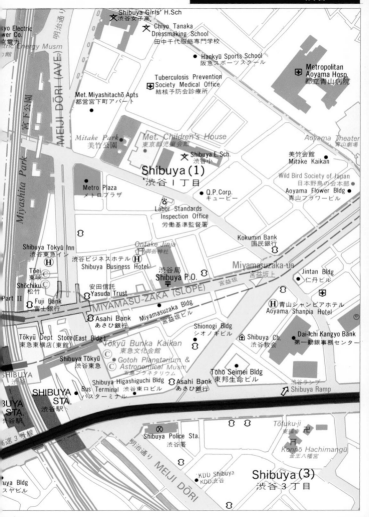

Shibuya Girls' H.Sch
渋谷女子高

Chiyo Tanaka
Dressmaking School
田中千代服飾専門学校

Hankyū Sports School
阪急スポーツスクール

Tuberculosis Prevention
Society Medical Office
結核予防会診療所

Metropolitan
Aoyama Hosp.
都立青山病院

ᴋyo Electric
wer Co.
ric Energy Musm

Met. Miyashitachō Apts
都営宮下町アパート

Mitake Park
美竹公園

Met. Children's House
東京都児童会館

Aoyama Theater
青山劇場

Miyashita Park

Shibuya E. Sch.
渋谷小

Mitake Kaikan
美竹会館

Shibuya (1)
渋谷1丁目

Metro Plaza
メトロプラザ

Q.P. Corp.
キューピー

Wild Bird Society of Japan
日本野鳥の会本部

Aoyama Flower Bldg
青山フラワービル

Labor Standards
Inspection Office
労働基準監督署

Kokumin Bank
国民銀行

Ontake Jinja
御嶽神社

Shibuya Tōkyū Inn
渋谷東急イン

渋谷ビジネスホテル
Shibuya Business Hotel

Tōei
東映

Shibuya P.O.
渋谷局

Miyamasuzaka-ue
宮益坂上

Jintan Bldg
仁丹ビル

Shōchiku
松竹

安田信託
Yasuda Trust

宮益坂
Miyamasuzaka Bldg
宮益坂ビル

Part II

Fuji Bank
富士銀行

MIYAMASU-ZAKA (SLOPE)

青山シャンピアホテル
Aoyama Shanpia Hotel

Asahi Bank
あさひ銀行

Shionogi Bldg
シオノギビル

Shibuya Ch.
渋谷教会

Dai-Ichi Kangyo Bank
第一勧銀事務センター

Tōkyū Dept Store (East Bldg)
東急東横店（東館）

Tōkyū Bunka Kaikan
東急文化会館

Gotoh Planetarium &
Astronomical Musm
五島プラネタリウム

Shibuya Tōkyū
渋谷東急

Toho Seimei Bldg
東邦生命ビル

Shibuya Ramp
渋谷ランプ

SHIBUYA
STA.

Shibuya Higashiguchi Bldg
渋谷東口ビル

Asahi Bank
あさひ銀行

BUYA
STA.
渋谷駅

Bus Terminal 渋谷東口
バスターミナル

SHIBUYA
STA.
渋谷駅

Shibuya Police Sta.
渋谷署

Tōfuku-ji
東福寺

Konnō Hachimangū
金王八幡宮

Shibuya (3)
渋谷3丁目

MEIJI DORI

KDD Shibuya
KDD渋谷

ᴜya Bldg
ヤビル

Tōgō Jinja (shrine)
東郷神社

Tōgō Mem. Hall
東郷記念館

Rehabilitation C
Phys

TAKESHITA DŌRI

原宿駅

竹下通り

Palais France
パレフランス

MEIJI DŌRI (AVE.) 明治通り

Jingūmae (1)
神宮前 1 丁目

原宿クエスト
Harajuku Quest

Ota Mem. Mus. of Art
太田記念美術館

MEIJI-JINGŪMAE

Laforet Harajuku

Jing
神宮

Kyu Shibuya River Promenade

Corp Olympia
コープオリンピア

Harajuku Tower Height
原宿タワーハイツ

Emb. of Portugal
ポルトガル大使館

Jingūmae
神宮前

OMOTE SANDO (AVE.)

Central Apts
セントラルアパート

Tin Toy Musm
ちちゃの博物館

Japan Int'l Sch.
ジャパンインターナショナル

Jingūmae E. Sch.
神宮前小

Jingūmae (6)
神宮前 6 丁目

Harajuku-ekimae P.O.
原宿駅前局

Kiddy Land
キディランド

Jingubashi Bldg
神宮橋ビル

Dōgenkai Aoyama
同潤会青山アパ

Oriental Bazaar
オリエンタルバザー

Nurse's Agency
看護協会

Tokyo Union Ch.
東京ユニオン教会

Kirin Brewery (H.O.)
キリンビール本社

Kyōcera Yashika Bldg
京セラヤシカビル

卍 Chōsen-ji

Kyu Shibuya River Promenade

Tenriism Shrine
天理教会

Har

Ⓗ Corp Inn Shibuya
コープイン渋谷

YAMANOTE LINE 山手線

Jingūdōri Park 神宮通公園

Onden Jinja
穏田神社

Jingūmae (5)
神宮前 5 丁目

Kita-Aoyama
北青山

MEIJI DŌRI (AVE.) 明治通り

Shibuya Girls' H. Sch.
渋谷女子高

SHIBUYA-KU
渋谷区

Chiyo Tanaka Dressmaking Sch
東京田中千代服飾専門学校

Met. Aoyama Hosp.
都立青山病院

JBP C
JBPオ

国連大学
United Nations Univ

Nat'l Children's Castle
(Kodomo-no-shiro)
こどもの城

渋谷
Shibuya (1)

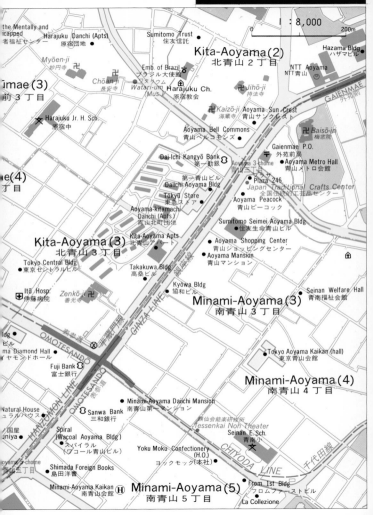

1 : 8,000

0　　　　　　　　　200m

the Mentally and
Handicapped
者福祉センター

Harajuku Danchi (Apts)
原宿団地

Sumitomo Trust
住友信託

Kita-Aoyama(2)
北青山 2 丁目

Hazama Bldg
ハザマビル

Myōen-ji
妙円寺

Emb. of Brazil
ブラジル大使館

NTT Aoyama
NTT青山

GAIENMAE
外苑前

imae(3)
前 3 丁目

Chōan-ji
長安寺

Watari-um
Mus.
ワタリウム美

Harajuku Ch.
原宿教会

Jihō-ji
持法寺

Harajuku Jr. H. Sch.
原宿中

Kaizō-ji
海蔵寺

Aoyama Sun-Crest
青山サンクレスト

Baisō-in
梅窓院

e(4)
丁目

Aoyama Bell Commons
青山ベルコモンズ

Gaienmae P.O.
外苑前局

Dai-Ichi Kangyō Bank
第一勧銀

Aoyama 3-chome
青山三丁目

Aoyama Metro Hall
青山メトロ会館

Daiichi Aoyama Bldg
第一青山ビル

Plaza 246

Japan Traditional Crafts Center
全国伝統的工芸品センター

Tōkyū Store
東急ストア

Aoyama Peacock
青山ピーコック

Aoyama-kitamachi
Danchi (Apts)
青山北町団地

Sumitomo Seimei Aoyama Bldg
住友生命青山ビル

Kita-Aoyama Apts
北青山アパート

Aoyama Shopping Center
青山ショッピングセンター

Kita-Aoyama(3)
北青山 3 丁目

Aoyama Mansion
青山マンション

Tokyo Central Bldg
東京セントラルビル

Takakuwa Bldg
高桑ビル

Itō Hosp.
伊藤病院

Zenkō-ji
善光寺

Kyowa Bldg
協和ビル

Seinan Welfare Hall
青南福祉会館

Minami-Aoyama(3)
南青山 3 丁目

OMOTESANDO
表参道

ma Diamond Hall
イヤモンドホール

Fuji Bank
富士銀行

Tokyo Aoyama Kaikan (hall)
東京青山会館

Minami-Aoyama(4)
南青山 4 丁目

Natural House
ラルハウス

Minami-Aoyama Daiichi Mansion
南青山第一マンション

屋
uniya

Sanwa Bank
三和銀行

Tessenkai Noh Theater

Seinan E. Sch.
青南小

Spiral
(Wacoal Aoyama Bldg)
スパイラル
(ワコール青山ビル)

Yoku Moku Confectionery
(H.O.)
ヨックモック(本社)

oyama 3-chome
丁目

Shimada Foreign Books
島田洋書

Minami-Aoyama Kaikan
南青山会館

Minami-Aoyama(5)
南青山 5 丁目

From 1st Bldg
フロムファーストビル

La Collezione

CHIYODA LINE
千代田線

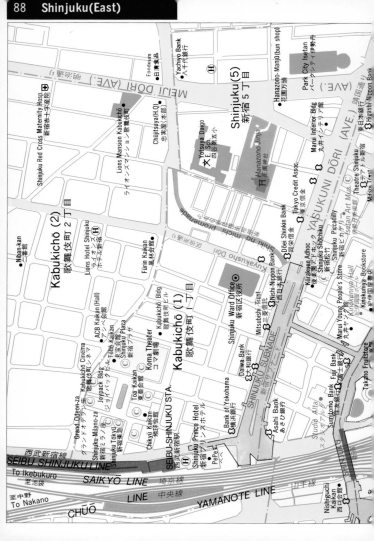

Shinjuku Gyoen
(Shinjuku Imperial Gardens)
新宿御苑

I : 6,000

I : 6,000

200m

Shinjuku(2)
新宿二丁目

Shinjuku Dori 新宿通
SHINJUKU DORI (AVE.)

GYOEN

Shinjuku-gyoen Tunnel 新宿御苑トンネル

Shinjuku Hosp.
新宿病院

Asahi Bank
あさひ銀行

Shinjuku Scala-za
新宿スカラ座

Suehiro-tei storytellers' hall
末広亭

Sanwa Bank
三和銀行

Mitsubishi Bank
三菱銀行

Marui Meits Bldg.
丸井メンズ館

Naitōchō
内藤町

Tobi
新宿郵便局

Shinjuku Music Store
Kotani コタニ

Mt. Shinjuku
H. Sch.
都立新宿高

Saikyō Shinkin Bank
西京信金

卍 Tenryū-ji
天龍寺

Shinjuku(4)
新宿四丁目

Mitsubishi
Bank
三菱銀行
前

Marui Fashion Bldg
丸井ファッション館

WINS Shinjuku
ウインズ新宿

Nittsu
日通

Yoshida Bldg
吉田ビル

Central Hotel
セントラルホテル

Showakan
昭和館

Shinjuku(3)
新宿三丁目

Mitsukoshi
Dept Store
三越デパート

Musashino Kan
武蔵野館

Toyo Trust
東洋信託

Shinjuku Kokusai Theater
新宿国際劇場

Tokai Bank
東海銀行

Katsuraya Ryokan (H)
(Inn)桂屋旅館

Sendagaya
千駄ヶ谷

To Yotsuya, Shibuya
至四ッ谷 渋谷

CHUO LINE 中央線

YAMANOTE LINE 山手線

KŌSHŪ KAIDŌ (AVE.)
甲州街道

TOEI SHINJUKU LINE 都営新宿線

SHINJUKU STA.
新宿駅

Central Entrance
中央口

My City
マイシティ

SHINJUKU STA.
新宿駅

South Entrance
南口

Lumine 2

MYLOAD
ルミネ

ODAKYU LINE 小田急線

Miyako Bldg
ミヤコビル

Shinjuku JR Bldg
新宿JRビル

ODAKYU LINE

KEIO LINE 京王線

Keio Dept Store
京王デパート

Lumine

Mitsubishi
Bank
三菱銀行

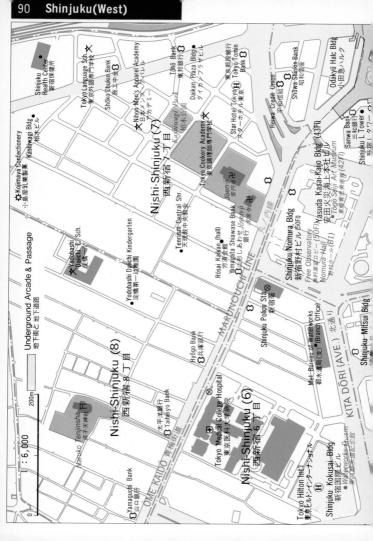

Nishi-Shinjuku (7)
西新宿 7 丁目

Nishi-Shinjuku (8)
西新宿 8 丁目

Nishi-Shinjuku (6)
西新宿 6 丁目

1 : 6,000

0 ——— 200m

Underground Arcade & Passage
地下街と地下通路

Shinjuku Health Center
新宿保健所

Kojimaya Confectionery
小島屋乳業菓

Kashiwagi Bldg
柏木ビル

Tokyo Language Sch
東京外語専門学校

Nihon Men's Apparel Academy
日本メンズ・アパレミー

Shōkō Chūkin Bank
商工中金

Tōhō Bank
東邦銀行

東京都民銀行 Tokyo Tomin Bank

Daikan Plaza Bldg
ダイカンプラザビル

Star Hotel Tokyo
スターホテル東京

Tokyo Cookery Academy
東京調理師専門学校

Joen-ji
常円寺

Jōsen-ji
常泉寺

Kōshū Kaidō 甲州街道

Heiwa Credit Union
平和信組

Shōwa Shinkin Bank
昭和信金

Odakyū Halc Bldg
小田急ハルク

Sanwa Bank
三和銀行

Shinjuku L Tower
新宿Lタワービル

Shinjuku-Mitsui Bldg
新宿三井ビル

Shinjuku Nomura Bldg
新宿野村ビル

Free Observatory
無料展望台 (50F)

Yasuda Kasai-Kaijo Bldg (43Fl)
安田火災海上本社ビル

Nomura Hall
Nomura Hall(B1)

Togo Seiji Art Museum
東郷青児美術館(42Fl)

Yodobashi Daiichi Sch.
淀橋第一小

Yodobashi Daiichi Kindergarten
淀橋第一幼稚園

Tenrism Central Shr.
天理教新宿中央教会

Risai Kaikan (hall)
労働衛生

Yamagata Shiawase Bank
山形しあわせ銀行

Shinjuku Police Sta
新宿署

MARUNOUCHI LINE

Shinjuku Police Sta
新宿署

Naruko Tenjinsha
成子天神社

Ome Kaido 青梅街道

Ōhei Bank
大平洋銀行

Taiheiyo Bank

Hyōgo Bank
兵庫銀行

Met. Bureau of Waterworks
都水道局(支)(Branch Office)

Tokyo Medical College Hospital
東京医科大学病院

Nishi-Shinjuku (6)
西新宿 6 丁目

Tokyo Hilton Int'l
東京ヒルトン・インターナショナル

Shinjuku Kokusai Bldg
新宿国際ビル

Waterworks Museum
東京都水道記念館

Yamaguchi Bank
山口銀行

Kita Dōri (Ave.)
北通り

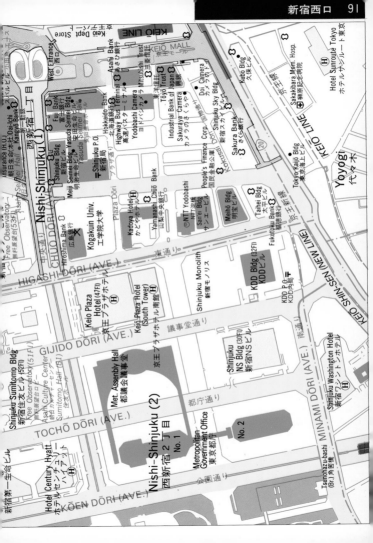

Ikebukuro (2)
池袋2丁目

I : 60,000

0   200m

Ikebukuru

Sugamo Shinkin Bank
巣鴨信金

Tokiwa Dōri (Ave.) ときわ通り

Ikebukuro P.O
池袋局

Higashi Nippon Bank
東日本銀行

Ōkubo Hosp.
大久保病院

Taiheiyō Bank
太平洋銀行

Hotel Kyōt
ホテル京都

Hote
ホテ

Rosa Kaikan (hall)
ロサ会館

Dai-Ichi Inn
Ikebukuro
第一イン池袋

Gunma Bank
群馬銀行

Cinema Rosa
シネマロサ

Ni
日

Sumitomo Bank
住友銀行

Scala-z
スカラ

Hotel Suncity
ホテルサンシティ

Tōkyū
東急

Yōkado Bldg
ヨーカ堂ビル

Sumitomo Trust
住友信託

Tōkai
東海

丸井

Tōyō Trust
東洋信託

Dai-Ichi Kangyō Bank
第一勧銀

North Entrance
北口

Mitsukos
三越s

Hōrindō Bookstore
芳林堂書店

Ikebukuro Parco Store
池袋パルコ

Sanwa
三和銀

Marui Dept Store
丸井

West Entrance
西口
Tōbu Dept Store
東武デパート

TŌBU
IKEBUKURO
STA. 東武

Fuji Bank
富士銀行

Ikebukuro
Nishiguchi Park
池袋西口公園

Fuji Bank
富士銀行

Mitsubishi Trust
三菱信託

East Entrance
東口

Yas

Tokyo Metropolitan Art Space
東京芸術劇場

JR
IKEBUKURO
STATION
池袋駅

Nishi-Ikebukuro (1)
西池袋1丁目

South Entrance
南口

Tokyo Nishiikebukuro Bldg
東京西池袋ビル

Plaza Metropolitan
プラザメトロポリタン

Kinkadō St
キンカ堂

(Tōbu Dept Store)
(東武デパート)

Hotel Metropolitan
ホテルメトロポリタン

Seibu Dept Store
西武デパート

Shōkō Chūkin
Bank 商工金

SEIBU IKEBUKURO
STA. 西武池袋駅

Seibu SMABldg
西武SMA館

WAVE

Sezon Musm of Art
セゾン美術館

Theatre Ikebukuro
テアトル池袋

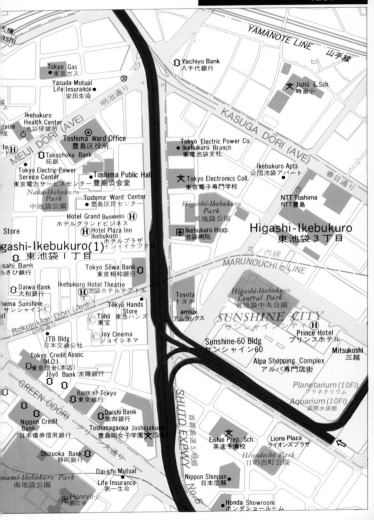

YAMANOTE LINE　山手線

8 Yachiyo Bank
八千代銀行

文 Jishū E. Sch.
時習小

Tokyo Gas
●東京ガス

Yasuda Mutual
Life Insurance ●
安田生命

KASUGA DORI (AVE)

Ikebukuro
Health Center
池袋保健所

Tokyo Electric Power Co.
● Ikebukuro Branch
東電池袋支社

Ikebukuro Apts
公団池袋アパート

H Toshima Ward Office
豊島区役所

8 Takushoku Bank
拓銀

文 Tokyo Electronics Coll.
東京電子専門学校

Tokyo Electric Power
Service Center
東京電力サービスセンター 豊島公会堂

● Toshima Public Hall

NTT Toshima
NTT豊島

*Naka-Ikebukuro
Park*
中池袋公園

Toshima Ward Center
● 豊島区民センター

*Higashi-Ikebukuro
Park*
東池袋公園

Hotel Grand Business **H**
ホテルグランドビジネス

H Hotel Plaza Inn
Ikebukuro
ホテルプラザ
イン・イケブクロ

✚ Ikebukuro Hosp.
池袋病院

**Higashi-Ikebukuro
東池袋 3 丁目**

gashi-Ikebukuro(1)
東池袋 1 丁目

MARUNOUCHI LINE
丸ノ内線

shi Bank
さし銀行

Tokyo Sōwa Bank
東京相和銀行

8 Daiwa Bank
大和銀行

Ikebukuro Hotel Theatre
池袋ホテルテアトル

Toyota
トヨタ

*Higashi-Ikebukuro
Central Park*
池袋中央公園

H池袋ホテルテアトル

nema Sunshine
サンシャイン

SUNSHINE CITY
サンシャインシティ

Store

Ⓒ Tōkyū Hands
Store
東急ハンズ

amlux
アムラックス

Prince Hotel
プリンスホテル

Rokugokkar Dori (Ave)

Ⓒ Tōhō 東宝

Ⓒ Joy Cinema
ジョイシネマ

Sunshine-60 Bldg
サンシャイン60

Mitsukoshi
三越

JTB Bldg
日本交通公社

Alpa Shopping Complex
アルパ専門店街

Tokyo Credit Assoc.
(H.O.)
8 東京信全(本店)

Planetarium (10Fl)
プラネタリウム

8 Jōyō Bank 常陽銀行

Aquarium (10Fl)
国際水族館

8 Bank of Tokyo
東京銀行

GREEN ODORI

SHUTO EXPWY No.5
首都高速5号線

8 Nippon Credit
Bank
日本債券信用銀行

8 Daishi Bank
第四銀行

Toshimagaoka Joshigakuen
豊島岡女子学園文(SchI)

文 Eishin Prep. Sch.
英進予備校

Lions Plaza
ライオンズプラザ

Shizuoka Bank **8**
静岡銀行

Hinodecho Park
日の出町公園

nami-Ikebukuro Park
南池袋公園

Dai-ichi Mutual
Life Insurance
第一生命

Nippon Shinpan
日本信販

卍 Honryu-ji
本立寺

● Honda Showroom
ホンダショールーム

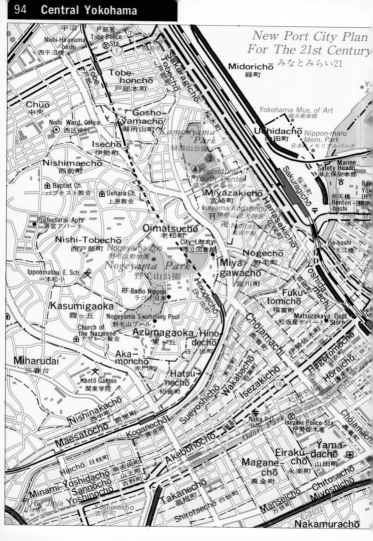

*New Port City Plan
For The 21st Century* みなとみらい21

Midorichō
緑町

Tobe Police Sta.

平沼
Nishi-Hiranuma
-bashi
西平沼橋

戸部署
Tobe Police
Sta.

Tobe-
honchō
戸部本町

Yokohama Mus. of Art
横浜美術館

Uchidachō
内田町

*Nippon-maru
Mem. Park*
日本丸メモリアルパーク

Chūō
中央

Nishi Ward Office
西区役所

Gosho-
yamachō
御所山町

*Kamon'yama
Park*
掃部山公園

*Marine
Headq.*
海上保安部

*Safety
Headq.*

Isechō
伊勢町

Nishimaechō
西前町

②
④ *Prefectural
Youth Center*
神奈川県青少年センター

Miyazakichō
宮崎町

Hanasakichō
花咲町

Baptist Ch.
バプテスト教会

Uehara Ch.
上原教会

伊勢山皇大神宮

Narita Ch.
成田山別院

Nogechō
野毛町

Prefectural Apts
県営アパート

Oimatsuchō
老松町

City Library
市立図書館

Miya-
gawachō
宮川町

Nishi-Tobechō
西戸部町

Nogeyama Zoo
野毛山動物園

Fuku-
tomichō
福富町

Ipponmatsu E. Sch.
一本松小

Nogeyama Park
野毛山公園

RF Radio Nippon
ラジオ日本

**Matsuzakaya Dept.
Store**
松坂屋デパート

Kasumigaoka
霞ヶ丘

Nogeyama Swimming Pool
野毛山プール

Azumagaoka
東ヶ丘

Hino-
dechō
日ノ出町

Chōjamachi
長者町

**Church of
the Nazarene**
ナザレン教会

Miharudai
三春台

Aka-
monchō
赤門町

Hatsu-
nechō
初音町

Wakabachō
若葉町

Hagoromochō
羽衣町

Hōraichō
蓬莱町

Kantō Gakuin
関東学院

Isezakichō
伊勢佐木町

Chōjamachi
長者町

Nishinakachō
西中町

Sueyoshichō
末吉町

Naka P.O.
中郵便局

Isezaki Police Sta.
伊勢佐木警察

Maesatochō
前里町

Koganechō
黄金町

Akebonochō
曙町

Odōri
大通り

Eiraku-
chō
永楽町

Yama-
dachō
山田町

Hiechō
日枝町

Magane-
chō
真金町

Little India

Minami-Yoshidachō
南吉田町

Sannōchō
山王町

Yoshinochō
吉野町

Manseichō
万世町

Chitosechō
千歳町

Miyoshichō
三吉町

Takanechō
高根町

Shirotaechō
白妙町

Nakamurachō
中村町

1 : 20,000

0   500m

Pacifico Yokohama
横浜国際平和会議場

Shinkō Futō (wharf)
新港ふ頭

Cosmoworld
コスモワールド

Grand Pier
(Ōsanbashi Futō)
大さん橋ふ頭

Shinkōchō
新港町

Bankoku-bashi (Br.)
万国橋

Shinkō-bashi (Br.)
新港橋

International
Passenger Terminal
国際船客ターミナルビル

Yüsen Bldg.
郵船ビル

an-dori
Motohamacho
元浜町

Kitanaka-dori
北仲通

Hon-chō
本町

haminaka-dori
南仲通

Yokohama Customshouse
横浜税関

Marine Police Sta.
水上署

Yamashita Futō
山下ふ頭

Kanagawa
NHK Pref. Office
神奈川県庁

Hikawa-maru
氷川丸

Silk Center
Trade Center
シルクセンター

Yamashita Park
山下公園

ai Hall
ホール

Courthouse
裁判所

Yokohama
Port P.O.
横浜港郵便局

Kenmin Hall
県民ホール

Bank of Japan
日本銀行

Nihon-Ōdori
日本大通

Naka Ward
Office
中区役所

Yama-
shitacho
山下町

The Hotel Yokohama
ザ・ホテルヨコハマ

Hotel New Grand
ホテルニューグランド

Yokohama City Office
横浜市役所

Kagachō
Police Sta.
加賀町署

Satellite Hotel
サテライト

Star Hotel
スターホテル

Yokohama
Park
横浜公園

Yokohama
Stadium
横浜スタジアム

China Town
(Chūka-gai)
中華街

Holiday Inn
ホリデイ・イン

Marine Tower
マリンタワー

Yamashitachō Ramp
山下町ランプ

YMCA
日本大通

Minato H. Sch.
港高校

Seaman's Hall
海員会館

Yūbin Chokin Kaikan
郵便貯金会館

Bund Hotel
バンドホテル

Minato Comm. H. Sch.
港商業高校

Aster Hotel
アスターホテル

TVK
テレビ神奈川

Yokohama Central Hosp.
横浜中央病院

Motomachi
元町

Meteorological Observatory
気象台

Courthouse
裁判所

Ogimachi
扇町

ko-kaeri
hip

Kotobukicho
寿町

Yoshi-
hamachō
吉浜町

Foreigners' Cemetery
外国人墓地

Minatono
mieruoka Park
港の見える丘公園

Matsukagecho
松影町

Motomachi
Park
元町公園

Yokonama Int'l Sch.
横浜インターナショナルスクール

Ferris Girls' Sch.
フェリス女学院

Suwa-
chō
諏訪町

Yokohama
Girls' (Comm.) H. Sch.
横浜女子商業高校

Yamatecho
山手町

Yamate Hosp.
山手病院

St. Joseph College
セント・ジョセフ・カレッジ

Ishikawacho
石川町

Yokohama Girls' H. Sch.
横浜女子高校

Yamate Catholic Ch.
山手カトリック教会

Futaba Gakuen
雙葉学園

St. Maur Int'l Sch.
サンモール・インターナショナルスクール

hikoshi

Kyōritsu Gakuen (Sch.)
共立学園

Ferris Women's Coll.
フェリス女学院大学

Kitamura Park
北村公園

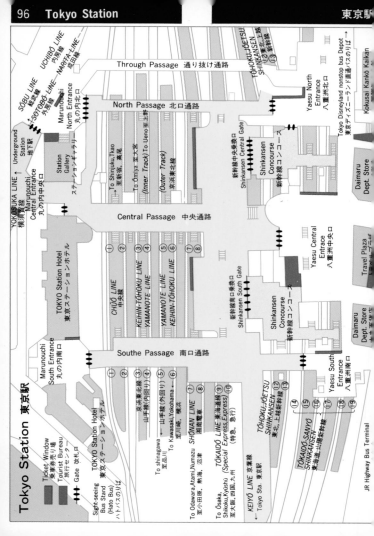

Useful Telephone Numbers
電話べんりページ

Usefull Information　主要案内

Tourist Information Center
ツーリスト・インフォメーション・センター
Tokyo (Yūrakuchō)　東京(有楽町)
　　　　　　　　　　　　　　(03)3502-1461
　Asakusa　浅草　　　　　　(03)3842-5566
　Yokohama　横浜　　　　　(045)641-4759
　Narita Airport　成田空港　(0476)32-8711
Tourist Service　観光案内
　English tape　英語　　　　(03)3503-2911
　French tape　仏語　　　　(03)3503-2926
Japan Travel-Phones (toll free)　旅行相談
　Eastern Japan　東日本　　0120-222-800
　Western Japan　西日本　　0120-444-800
Flight Information　フライト案内
　Narita　成田　　　　　　　(0476)32-2800
　Haneda　羽田　　　　　　(03)3747-8010
Airport Limousine Bus Information
　空港リムジンバス案内　　　(03)3665-7232
Keisei Skyliner Information
　京成スカイライナー案内　　(03)3831-0131
Japan Travel-Bureau　日本交通公社
　　　　　　　　　　　　　　(03)3276-7777

Telephone　電話
　Long Distance Calls (operator-assisted)
　市外通話　　　　　　　　　　　　　100
　Collect／Credit Calls
　コレクト／クレジット通話　　　　　106

Number Inquiries　電話番号案内
　　　　　　(03)3277-1010(English)or104
International Telephone　国際電話
　Booking (operator-assisted calls)
　申し込み　　　　　　　　　　　　0051
　Inquiries (operator-assisted calls)
　問い合わせ　　　　　　　　　　　0057
Telegram　電報
　Domestic　国内　　　　　　　　　115
　International　国際　　　(03)3344-5151
Police　警察への急報　　　　　　　　110
Fire and Ambulance (calls answered in japanese)
　火事、救急車　　　　　　　　　　119
Hospital Information　病院案内　(03)3212-2323
American Pharmacy (English spoken)
　アメリカン・ファーマシー　(03)3271-4034
Tokyo English Life Line
　東京イングリッシュ・ライフ・ライン
　　　　　　　　　　　　　　(03)3264-4347
Foreign Residents' Advisory Center (Tokyo)
　東京都庁外国人相談センター　(03)5320-7744
Tokyo Central Post Office
　東京中央郵便局　　　　　　(03)3284-9539
Tokyo International Post Office
　東京国際郵便局　　　　　　(03)3241-4869
Tokyo Regional Immigration Bureau
　東京入国管理局　　　　　　(03)3213-8111

Museums　博物館

Ancient Orient Museum
　古代オリエント博物館　　(03)3989-3491
Asakusa Handicrafts Museum　浅草巧芸館
　　　　　　　　　　　　(03)3845-3591　⑦
Asakusa Museum　浅草風俗歴史館
　　　　　　　　　　　　(03)3844-5656　⑦
Bunka Gakuen Costume Museum
　文化学園服飾博物館　　(03)3299-2387　㊳
Communications Museum　通信総合博物館
　　　　　　　　　　　　(03)3244-6811　㊸
Costume Museum　杉野学園衣裳博物館
　　　　　　　　　　　　(03)3491-8151　㊻
Daimyō Clock Museum　大名時計博物館
　　　　　　　　　　　　(03)3821-6913　㊱
Fuchū Municipal Museum Kyōdonomori
　府中郷土の森　　　　　(0423)68-7921
Fukagawa Edo Museum　深川江戸資料館
　　　　　　　　　　　　(03)3630-8625
Gas Science Center　ガスの科学館
　　　　　　　　　　　　(03)3534-1111
Gotoh Planetarium　五島プラネタリウム
　　　　　　　　　　　　(03)3407-7409　㊺
Japan Folk Crafts Museum　日本民芸館
　　　　　　　　　　　　(03)3467-4527　㉒
Japan Traditional Crafts Center
　全国伝統的工芸品センター(03)3403-2460　㊲
Japanese Sake Center　日本酒センター
　　　　　　　　　　　　(03)3575-0656　㊿
Japanese Sword Museum　刀剣博物館
　　　　　　　　　　　　(03)3379-1386

Kanagawa pref. Museum　神奈川県立博物館
　　　　　　　　　　　　(045)201-0926　㊾
Kawasaki Municipal Park of Japanese Houses
　日本民家園　　　　　　(044)922-2181　⑪
Mus. of Maritime Science　船の科学館
　　　　　　　　　　　　(03)3528-1111　⑦
Mus. of Modern Japanese Literature
　日本近代文学館　　　　(03)3466-5150
Nat'l Science Museum　国立科学博物館
　　　　　　　　　　　　(03)3822-0111　㊱
NHK Broadcast Museum　NHK放送博物館
　　　　　　　　　　　　(03)3433-5211　㊼
Paper Museum　紙の博物館　(03)3911-3545　㉑
Shitamachi Museum　下町風俗資料館
　　　　　　　　　　　　(03)3823-7461　⑦
Science Museum　科学技術館
　　　　　　　　　　　　(03)3212-8471　㊶
Sunshine Planetarium　サンシャインプラネタリ
　ウム　　　　　　　　　(03)3989-3466　㉞
Taitō Traditional Crafts Museum
　台東区伝統工芸展示館　(03)3847-2587　⑦
Tokyo Met. Mus. of Modern Literature
　東京都近代文学博物館　(03)3466-5150
Tokyo Met. Takao Mus. of Natural History
　高尾自然科学博物館　　(0426)61-0305　⑬
Tokyo National Museum　東京国立博物館
　　　　　　　　　　　　(03)3822-1111　㊱
Transportation Museum　交通博物館
　　　　　　　　　　　　(03)3251-8481　⑦

Zoological Garden, Aquarium, Botanical Garden
動物園・水族館・植物園

Horikiri-Shōbuen 堀切菖蒲園　(03)3697-5237　⑥
Inokashira Natural Cultural Garden
　井の頭自然文化園　　　(0422)43-2566　⑩
Keiō Hyakkaen　京王百花苑　(0424)82-2653　⑪
Koishikawa Botanical Garden　小石川植物園
　　　　　　　　　　　　(03)3814-0138　㉞
Makino Memorial Garden　牧野記念庭園
　　　　　　　　　　　　(03)3922-2920
Nat'l Garden Shinjuku-gyoen　新宿御苑

　　　　　　　　　　　　(03)3350-0151　㊴
Nati'l Park for Nature Study　国立自然教育園
　　　　　　　　　　　　(03)3441-7176　㊻
Sunshine Aquarium
　サンシャイン国際水族館　(03)3989-3466　㉞
Tama Forest Science Garden　多摩森林科学園
　　　　　　　　　　　　(0426)61-1121　⑬
Tokyo Met. Jindai Botanical Park
　東京都神代植物公園　　(0424)83-2300　⑩

Tokyo Met. Tama Zoological Park
東京都多摩動物公園 (0425)91-1611 ⓫
Tokyo Met. Ueno Zoological Gardens
東京都上野動物園 (03)3828-5171 ㊱
Tokyo Met. Yumenoshima Tropical Plant Dome
東京都夢の島熱帯植物館 (03)3522-0281 ❼
Tokyo Sea Life Park 葛西臨海水族園
(03)3869-5151 ❼
Tokyo Tower Aquarium 東京タワー水族館
(03)3434-8833 (52)
Yomiuri Land Aquarium
読売ランド海水水族館 (044)966-1111 ⓫

Art Museums 美術館

Asakura Choso Museum 朝倉彫塑館
(03)3821-4549 ㉚
Bridgestone Mus. of Art ブリジストン美術館
(03)3563-0241 (70)
Bunkamura 東急文化村 (03)3477-9252 (84)
Gotoh Art Museum 五島美術館
(03)3703-0661
Hara Mus. of Contemporary Art 原美術館
(03)3445-0651 (59)
Hatakeyama Collection 畠山記念館
(03)3447-5787
Idemitsu Art Gallery 出光美術館
(03)3213-9402 (61)
Itabashi Ward Art Museum 板橋区立美術館
(03)3979-3251
Iwasaki Chihiro Art Mus. of Picture Books
いわさきちひろ絵本美術館 (03)3995-0612
Kurita Museum 栗田美術館 (03)3666-6246
Machida City Mus. of Graphic Arts
町田市立国際版画美術館 (0427)26-2771
Matsuoka Art Museum 松岡美術館
(03)3431-8284
Meiji Mem, Picture Gallery 聖徳記念絵画館
(03)3401-5179 ㊺
Meguro Ward Art Mus. 目黒美術館
(03)3714-1201
Mus. of Calligraphy 書道美術館 (03)3872-2645
Nat'l Film Center 国立近代美術館フィルムセンター (03)3214-2561
Nat'l Mus. of Modern Art, Tokyo
東京国立近代美術館 (03)3214-2561 ㊶
Nat'l Mus. of Western Art 国立西洋美術館
(03)3828-5131 (76)
Nezu Art Museum 根津美術館
(03)3400-2536 (51)
O Art Museum O美術館 (03)3495-4040
Ōkura Museum 大倉集古館 (03)3583-0781 (83)
Ōta Memorial Mus. of Art 太田記念美術館
(03)3403-0880 (86)
Riccar Art Museum リッカー美術館
(03)3571-3254 (68)
Senshū Bunko 千秋文庫 (03)3261-0075
Setagaya Art Museum 世田谷美術館
(03)3415-6011 ㉒
Sezon Mus. of Art セゾン美術館
(03)5992-0155 (92)
Shōtō Art Museum 松涛美術館 (03)3465-9421
Sōgetsu Art Center 草月会館
(03)3408-1126 (80)
Sogō Mus. of Art そごう美術館 (045)465-2361
Striped House Museum
ストライプハウス美術館 (03)3405-8108
Suntory Mus. of Art サントリー美術館
(03)3470-1073 (64)
Tenri Gallery 天理ギャラリー (03)3292-7025
Togō Seiji Art Museum 東郷青児美術館
(03)3349-3081 (90)
Toguri Mus. of Art 戸栗美術館 (03)3465-0070
Tokyo Central Mus. of Art
東京セントラル美術館 (03)3564-0711 (69)
Tokyo International Art Museum
東京国際美術館 (0423)38-9731
Tokyo Met. Art Museum 東京都美術館
(03)3823-6921 ㊱
Tokyo Met. Mus. of Photography
東京都写真美術館 (03)3280-0031 (56)
Tokyo Met. Teien Art Museum
東京都庭園美術館 (03)3443-8500 (56)
Ueno Royal Museum 上野の森美術館
(03)3833-4191 ㊱
WATARI-UM Art Mus. ワタリウム美術館
(03)3402-3001
Yamatane Mus. of Art 山種美術館
(03)3669-7643 (71)
Yayoi Art Museum 弥生美術館
(03)3812-0012 ㉟
Yokohama Mus. of Art 横浜美術館
(045)221-0300 (94)
Yokoyama Taikan Mem. Cottege
横山大観記念館 (03)8321-1017

Libraries　図書館

British Council Library　ブリティッシュ・カウ
　ソシル図書館　　　　　　(03)3235-8031
Nat'l Archives　国立公文書館　(03)3214-0621
Nat'l Diet Library　国立国会図書館
　　　　　　　　　　　　(03)3581-2331 **66**

Tokyo Met. Central Library　都立中央図書館
　　　　　　　　　　　　(03)3442-8451 **52**
Tokyo Met. Hibiya Library　都立日比谷図書館
　　　　　　　　　　　　(03)3502-0101 **67**
Tōyō Bunko　東洋文庫　(03)3942-0121 **29**

Theaters, Halls　劇場，ホール

Aoyama Theater　青山劇場　(03)3797-5678 **50**
Asakusa public Hall　浅草公会堂
　　　　　　　　　　　　(03)3844-7491 **79**
Asakusa Tōhō (cinema)　浅草東宝 (映)
　　　　　　　　　　　　(03)3844-3141 **78**
Casals Hall　カザルスホール　(03)3294-1229 **74**
Chō-fu Green Hall　調布グリーンホール
　　　　　　　　　　　　(0424)81-7611
Fuchū-nomori Art Theater　府中の森芸術劇場
　　　　　　　　　　　　(0423)35-6211
Ginza Noh Theater　銀座能楽堂
　　　　　　　　　　　　(03)3571-0197 **68**
Hachiōji Civic Auditorium　八王子市民会館
　　　　　　　　　　　　(0426)22-8251
Hakuhinkan Theater　博品館劇場　(03)3571-1003
Haiyūza Theater　俳優座劇場　(03)3470-2880 **52**
Hibiya Eiga (cinema)　日比谷映画 (03)3591-5353
Hibiya Public Hall　日比谷公会堂
　　　　　　　　　　　　(03)3591-6388 **68**
Hōshō Noh Theater　宝生能楽堂　(03)3811-4843
Ikebukuro Scala-za (cinema)
　池袋スカラ座 (映)　　(03)3971-1977 **93**
Imperial Theater (Teikoku-gekijō)　帝国劇場
　　　　　　　　　　　　(03)3213-7221 **61**
Kabuki-za　歌舞伎座　　(03)3541-3131 **69**
Kanagawa Pref. Kenmin Hall
　神奈川県立県民ホール　(045)662-5901 **95**
Kanze Noh Theater　観世能楽堂
　　　　　　　　　　　　(03)3469-5241 **50**
Kita Roppeita Mem.Noh Theater
　喜多六平太記念能楽堂　(03)3491-7773
Marunouchi Piccadilly (cinema)
　丸の内ピカデリー (映)　(03)3201-2881 **69**
Nakano Sun Plaza　中野サンプラザ
　　　　　　　　　　　　(03)3388-1151 **20**

National Noh Theater 国立能楽堂 (03)3423-1331
National Theater　国立劇場　(03)3265-7411 **64**
NHK Hall　NHK ホール　(03)3465-1111 **50**
Nihon Theater　日本劇場　(03)3574-1131 **69**
Nihon Toshi Center Hall
　日本都市センターホール　(03)3265-8211 **64**
Nippon Budōkan 日本武道館 (03)3216-5100 **41**
Nissei Theater　日生劇場　(03)3503-3111 **68**
Orchard Hall　オーチャードホール
　　　　　　　　　　　　(03)3477-3208 **84**
Pacifico Yokohama　パシフィコ横浜
　　　　　　　　　　　　(045)221-2121 **95**
Parthénon Tama パルテノン多摩 (0423)75-1414
Shibuya Pantheon (cinema)
　渋谷パンテオン (映)　　(03)3407-7219
Shibuya Public Hall　渋谷公会堂
　　　　　　　　　　　　(03)3463-1211 **50**
Shinbashi Enbujō 新橋演舞場 (03)3541-2211 **47**
Shinjuku Bunka Center　新宿区立新宿文化セン
　ター　　　　　　　　(03)3350-1141 **39**
Shinjuku Koma Theater　新宿コマ劇場
　　　　　　　　　　　　(03)3202-8111 **88**
Shinjuku Milano-za (cinema)
　新宿ミラノ座 (映)　　(03)3202-1189 **88**
Shinjuku Piccadilly (cinema)
　新宿ピカデリー (映)　(03)3352-1771 **88**
Shinjuku Plaza (cinema)　新宿プラザ(映)
　　　　　　　　　　　　(03)3200-9141 **88**
Shinjuku Scala-za (cinema)　新宿スカラ座(映)
　　　　　　　　　　　　(03)3351-3127 **89**
Shinjuku Tōei (cimema)　新宿東映(映)
　　　　　　　　　　　　(03)3351-3060 **89**
Shōchiku Central (cinema)
　松竹セントラル(映)　　(03)3541-2714
Suginami Public Hall　杉並公会堂

(03)3398-1956 ⑳
Sugino Kōdō　杉野講堂　(03)3491-8151 (56)
Sunshine Theater　サンシャイン劇場　(03)3987-5281 (93)
Suntory Hall　サントリーホール　(03)3505-1001 (81)
Tokyo Bay NK Hall　東京ベイ NK ホール　(0473)55-7000
Tokyo Dōme　東京ドーム　(03)3811-2111 ㉟
Tokyo Kōsei nenkin Kaikan　東京厚生年金会館　(03)3356-1111 ㊴
Tokyo Met. Art Space　東京芸術劇場　(03)5391-2111 (92)
Tokyo Met. Festival Hall　東京文化会館　(03)3828-2111 (76)
Tokyo Takarazuka Theater　東京宝塚劇場　(03)3591-1711 (68)
Ueno Shōchiku (cinema)　上野松竹(映)　(03)3831-3136 (76)
Ueno Suzumoto Theater　上野鈴本演芸場　(03)3834-5906 (77)
Ueno Tōhō (cinema)　上野東宝(映)　(03)3831-3431 (76)
U-port kan'i-hoken Hall　ゆうぽうと簡易保険ホール　(03)3490-5111 (57)
Yarai Noh Theater　矢来能楽堂　(03)3268-7311
Yomiuri Hall　よみうりホール　(03)3231-0551
Yūrakuchō Asahi Hall　有楽町朝日ホール　(03)3284-0131 (69)

Sports Facilities, Amusement Parks
スポーツ施設・遊園地

Ariake Colosseum　有明コロシアム　(03)3529-3301 ⑦
Jingū Stadium　神宮球場　(03)3404-8999 ㊺
Kōdōkan　講道館　(03)3811-7151 ㉟
Kokugikan (Sumō Stadium)　国技館　(03)3623-5111 ㊸
Komazawa Olympic Park　駒沢オリンピック公園　(03)3421-6121
Kōrakuen Hall 後楽園ホール (03)3811-2111 ㊶
Kōrakuen Yūenchi　後楽園ゆうえんち　(03)3811-2111 ㊶
Mukōgaoka Amusement Park　向ヶ丘遊園　(044)911-4281
Nakayama Racecourse　中山競馬場　(0473)34-2222
Nat'l Nishigaoka Stadium　国立西が丘競技場　(03)3403-1151
Natiolal Children's Castle　こどもの城　(03)3797-5666 ㊿
National Children's Land　こどもの国　(045)961-2111 ⑪
National Stadium　国立競技場　(03)3403-1151 ㊺
National Yoyogi Gymnadium　国立代々木競技場　(03)3468-1171 ㊿
Nippon Budōkan 日本武道館 (03)3216-5100 ㊶
Ōi Racecourse　大井競馬場　(03)3763-2151
Pr. Chichibu Rugby Stadium　秩父宮ラグビー場　(03)3401-3881
Sapporo Plaza　サッポロプラザ　(0482)57-5151
Seibu Amusement Park　西武園ゆうえんち　(0429)22-1371
Seibu Lions Baseball Stadium　西武ライオンズ球場　(0429)25-1151
Sunrio Puroland　サンリオピューロランド　(0423)39-1111
Tama Tech　多摩テック　(0425)91-0820
Tokyo Budōkan　東京武道館　(03)5697-2111
Tokyo Disneyland　東京ディズニーランド　(0473)54-0001 ⑦
Tokyo Dome (Big Egg)　東京ドーム　(03)3811-2111 ㊶
Tokyo Met. Children's House　東京都児童会館　(03)3409-6361 (85)
Tokyo Racecourse　東京競馬場　(0423)63-3141 ⑪
Tokyo Summer Land　東京サマーランド　(0425)58-6511 ⑫
Toshima-en　としまえん　(03)3990-3131 ⑧
Tokyo Gymnadium　東京体育館　(03)5474-2111 ㊺
Yokohama Stadium　横浜スタジアム　(045)661-1251 (95)
Yomiuri Land　よみうりランド　(044)966-1111 ⑪
Yumenoshima Sports Center　夢の島総合体育館　(03)3521-7321

Embassies 大使館

Algeria アルジェリア	(03) 3711-2661
Argentina アルゼンチン	(03) 3592-0321
Australia オーストラリア	(03) 5232-4008 (52)
Austria オーストリア	(03) 3451-8281 (51)
Bangladesh バングラデシュ	(03) 3442-1501 (56)
Belgium ベルギー	(03) 3262-0191 ㊵
Bolivia ボリビア	(03) 3499-5441
Brazil ブラジル	(03) 3404-5211 ㊺
Britain (See United Kingdom)	(03) 3265-5511
Brunei ブルネイ	(03) 3447-7997 (57)
Bulgaria ブルガリア	(03) 3465-1021 ㊹
Burundi ブルンジ	(03) 3443-7321
Cameroon カメルーン	(03) 3496-4101
Canada カナダ	(03) 3408-2101 ㊻
Central African Rep. 中央アフリカ	(03) 5272-0011
Chili チリ	(03) 3452-7561
China 中華人民共和国	(03) 3403-3380 (52)
Colombia コロンビア	(03) 3440-6451 (56)
Costa Rica コスタリカ	(03) 3486-1812
Côte d'Ivoire コートジボアール	(03) 3499-7021
Cuba キューバ	(03) 3716-3112 (57)
Czechoslovakia チェコスロバキア	(03) 3400-8122 (51)
Denmark デンマーク	(03) 3496-3001 ㊿
Djibouti ジブチ	(03) 3496-6135
Dominican Rep. ドミニカ共和国	(03) 3499-6020
EC-Delegation 駐日 EC 委員会	(03) 3239-0441
Guinea ギニア	(03) 3769-0451
Haiti ハイチ	(03) 3486-7070
Honduras ホンジュラス	(03) 3409-1150
Hungary ハンガリー	(03) 3476-6061 ㊿
India インド	(03) 3262-2391 ㊶
Indonesia インドネシア	(03) 3441-4201 (56)
Iran イラン	(03) 3446-8011 (52)
Iraq イラク	(03) 3423-1727
Ireland アイルランド	(03) 3263-0695
Israel イスラエル	(03) 3264-0911 ㊵
Italy イタリア	(03) 3453-5291 (52)
Jordan ヨルダン	(03) 3580-5856
Kenya ケニア	(03) 3723-4006
Korea (South) 大韓民国	(03) 3452-7611 (52)
Kuwait クウェート	(03) 3455-0361 (52)
Laos ラオス	(03) 3778-1660 (52)
Lebanon レバノン	(03) 3580-1227
Liberia リベリア	(03) 3499-2451
Libya リビア	(03) 3441-7138
Luxembourg ルクセンブルク	(03) 3265-9621 ㊵
Ecuador エクアドル	(03) 3499-2800
Egypt エジプト	(03) 3770-8022 ㊿
El Salvador エルサルバドル	(03) 3499-4461
Ethiopia エチオピア	(03) 3718-1003
Fiji フィジー	(03) 3587-2038
Finland フィンランド	(03) 3442-2231 (52)
France フランス	(03) 3473-0171 (52)
Gabon ガボン	(03) 3448-9540 (56)
Germany ドイツ	(03) 3473-0151 (52)
Ghana ガーナ	(03) 3710-8831 (51)
Greece ギリシア	(03) 3403-0871
Guatemala グアテマラ	(03) 3400-1830
Madagascar マダガスカル	(03) 3446-7252
Malaysia マレーシア	(03) 3280-7601 ㊿
Mauritania モーリタニア	(03) 3449-3822
Mexico メキシコ	(03) 3581-1131 (65)
Micronesia ミクロネシア連邦	(03) 3585-5456
Mongolia モンゴル	(03) 3469-2088 ㊹
Morocco モロッコ	(03) 3478-3271 ㊺
Myanmar ミャンマー	(03) 3441-9291 (59)
Nepal ネパール	(03) 3705-5558
Netherlands オランダ	(03) 3431-5126 (53)
New Zealand ニュージーランド	(03) 3467-2271 ㊹
Nicaragua ニカラグア	(03) 3499-0400
Nigeria ナイジェリア	(03) 3468-5531
Norway ノルウェー	(03) 3440-2611 (51)
Oman オマーン	(03) 3402-0877 ㊺
Pakistan パキスタン	(03) 3454-4861 (52)
Panama パナマ	(03) 3499-3741
Papua New Guinea パプア・ニューギニア	(03) 3454-7801
Paraguay パラグアイ	(03) 3447-7496
Peru ペルー	(03) 3406-4240
Philippines フィリピン	(03) 3496-2731 ㊿
Poland ポーランド	(03) 3711-5224 (56)
Portugal ポルトガル	(03) 3400-7907

Qatar　カタール	(03) 3446-7561	
Romania　ルーマニア	(03) 3479-0311	
Russia　ロシア	(03) 3583-4224	
Rwanda　ルワンダ	(03) 3486-7800	
Saudi Arabia　サウジアラビア	(03) 3589-5241	
Senegal　セネガル	(03) 3464-8451	50
Singapore　シンガポール	(03) 3586-9111	52
Somalia　ソマリア	(03) 3442-7141	56
Spain　スペイン	(03) 3583-8531	46
Sri Lanka　スリランカ	(03) 3585-7431	
Sudan　スーダン	(03) 3406-0811	51
Sweden　スウェーデン	(03) 5562-5050	46
Switzerland　スイス	(03) 3473-0121	51
Syria　シリア	(03) 3586-8977	
Tanzania　タンザニア	(03) 3425-4531	
Thailand　タイ	(03) 3441-7352	56
Tunisia　チュニジア	(03) 3353-4111	
Turkey　トルコ	(03) 3470-5131	45
U.A.E.　アラブ首長国連邦	(03) 5489-0804	
United Kingdom　イギリス	(03) 3265-5511	40
Uruguay　ウルグアイ	(03) 3486-1888	
U.S.A.　アメリカ	(03) 3224-5000	46
Vatican City　ローマ法王庁	(03) 3263-6851	40
Venezuela　ベネズエラ	(03) 3409-1501	
Viet Nam　ベトナム	(03) 3466-3311	44
Yemen　イエメン	(03) 3499-7151	
Zaire　ザイール	(03) 3423-3981	44
Zambia　ザンビア	(03) 3445-1041	
Zimbabwe　ジンバブエ	(03) 3280-0331	52

Consulates　領事館

TOKYO　東京

Belize　ベリーズ	(03) 3403-6963	Seychelles　セイシェル	(03) 3561-8002
Cyprus　キプロス	(03) 3294-9124	South Africa　南アフリカ	(03) 3265-3366
Gambia　ガンビア	(03) 3447-7806	Swaziland　スワジランド	(03) 3864-2106
Iceland　アイスランド	(03) 3531-8776	Tonga　トンガ	(03) 3502-2371
Kiribati　キリバス	(03) 3201-3487	Western Somoa　西サモア	(03) 3211-7604
Maldives　モルジブ	(03) 3589-3311		

YOKOHAMA　横浜

Mali　マリ	(03) 3562-8256
Malta　マルタ	(03) 3434-0401
Mauritius　モーリシャス	(03) 3211-8569
Monaco　モナコ	(03) 3211-4994
Nauru　ナウル	(03) 3581-9277
Niger　ニジェール	(03) 3505-6371
San Marino　サンマリノ	(03) 3498-8427

Argentina　アルゼンチン	(045) 641-4194
Colombia　コロンビア	(045) 312-8461
Denmark　デンマーク	(045) 651-1591
Korea(South)　大韓民国	(045) 621-4531
Netherlands　オランダ	(045) 651-1661
Norway　ノルウェー	(045) 641-0141
Paraguay　パラグアイ	(045) 401-3431
Sweden　スウェーデン	(045) 320-5253

Airlines　航空会社

TOKYO　東京

Aeroflot Soviet Airlines (SU)　アエロフロート・ソビエト航空		(03) 3434-9681
Air France (AF)　エールフランス		(03) 3475-2211
Air India (AI)　エア・インディア		(03) 3214-1981
Airlanka (UL)　エアランカ		(03) 3573-4261
Air Nauru (ON)　エア・ナウル		(03) 3581-9271
Air New Zealand (TE)　ニュージーランド航空		(03) 3287-1641
Alitalia Airlines (AZ)　アリタリア航空		(03) 3580-2242
All Nippon Airways (NH)　全日空	Int'l 国際	(03) 3272-1212
	Domestic 国内	(03) 5489-8800

American Airlines (AA)　アメリカン航空　　　　　　　　　　　　　　(03)3214-2111
Biman Bangladesh Airlines (BG)　バングラデシュ航空　　　　　　　　(03)3593-1252
British Airways (BA)　英国航空　　　　　　　　　　　　　　　　　　(03)3593-8811
Canadian Airlines Int'l (CP)　カナディアン航空　　　　　　　　　　　(03)3281-7426
Cathay Pacific Airways (CX)　キャセイ・パシフィック航空　　　　　　(03)3504-1531
China Airlines (CI)　中華航空　　　　　　　　　　　　　　　　　　　(03)3436-1661
Civil Aviation of China (CA)　中国民航　　　　　　　　　　　　　　　(03)3505-2021
Delta Air Lines (DL)　デルタ航空　　　　　　　　　　　　　　　　　(03)5275-7000
Eqypt Air (MS)　エジプト航空　　　　　　　　　　　　　　　　　　　(03)3211-4521
Finnair (AY)　フィンランド航空　　　　　　　　　　　　　　　　　　(03)3222-6801
Garuda Indonesian Airways (GA)　ガルーダ・インドネシア航空　　　　(03)3593-1181
Iberia Airlines (IB)　イベリア航空　　　　　　　　　　　　　　　　　(03)3582-3631
Iran Air (IR)　イラン航空　　　　　　　　　　　　　　　　　　　　(03)3586-2101
Iraqi Airways (IA)　イラク航空　　　　　　　　　(03)3624-5501　(03)3586-5801
Japan Airlines (JL)　日本航空　　　　　Int'l 国際　(03)5489-1111　(03)3457-1181
　　　　　　　　　　　　　　　　　Domestic 国内 5489-2111　(03)3456-2111
Japan Air System (JD)　日本エアシステム　　　　　Int'l 国際　(03)3438-1155
　　　　　　　　　　　　　　　　　　　　　　　Domestic 国内　(03)3432-6111
Japan Asia Airways (EG)　日本アジア航空　　　　　　　　　　　　　(03)3455-7511
KLM Royal Dutch Airlines (KL)　KLM オランダ航空　　　　　　　　(03)3216-0771
Korean Air (KE)　大韓航空　　　　　　　　　　　　　　　　　　　(03)3211-3311
Lufthansa German Airlines (LH)　ルフトハンザ・ドイツ航空　　　　　(03)3580-2111
Malaysian Airline System (MH)　マレーシア航空　　　　　　　　　　(03)3503-5961
Nothwest Airlines (NW)　ノースウエスト・オリエント航空　　　　　　(03)3432-6000
Pakistan Int'l Airlines (PK)　パキスタン国際航空　　　　　　　　　　(03)3216-6511
Philippine Airlines (PR)　フィリピン航空　　　　　　　　　　　　　(03)3593-2421
Qantas Airways (QF)　カンタス・オーストラリア航空　　　　　　　　(03)3593-7000
Sabena Belgian World Airlines (SN)　サベナベルギー航空　　　　　　(03)3585-6151
Scandinavian Airlines (SK)　スカンジナビア航空　　　　　　　　　　(03)3503-8101
Singapore Airlines (SQ)　シンガポール航空　　　　　　　　　　　　(03)3213-3431
Swiss Air Transport (SR)　スイス航空　　　　　　　　　　　　　　(03)3212-1011
Thai Airways Int'l (TG)　タイ国際航空　　　　　　　　　　　　　　(03)3503-3311
United Airlines (UA)　ユナイテッド航空　　　　　　　　　　　　　(03)3817-4411
UTA French Airlines (UT)　UTA フランス航空　　　　　　　　　　(03)3593-0773
Varig Brazilian Airlines (RG)　ヴァリグ・ブラジル航空　　　　　　　(03)3211-6751

Hotels and Inns　ホテル・旅館

TOKYO　東京

Akasaka Prince H.　赤坂プリンスホテル　　　　　　　　(03)3234-1111 **64**
Akasaka Shanpia H.　赤坂シャンピアホテル　　　　　　　(03)3586-0811 **65**
Akasaka Tōkyū H.　赤坂東急ホテル　　　　　　　　　　　(03)3580-2311 **46**
Akihabara Washington H.　秋葉原ワシントンホテル　　　　(03)3255-3311
ANA H. Tokyo　東京全日空ホテル　　　　　　　　　　　(03)3505-1111 **81**
Aoi Grand H.　葵グランドホテル　　　　　　　　　　　　(03)3946-2721
Aoyama Shanpia H.　青山シャンピアホテル　　　　　　　(03)3407-2111 **85**
Asakusa View H.　浅草ビューホテル　　　　　　　　　　(03)3842-2111 **78**

Asia Center of Japan　アジア会館　　　　　　　　　　　(03) 3402-6111 **46**
Atagoyama Tōkyū Inn　愛宕山東急イン　　　　　　　　　(03) 3431-0109
Azabu City H.　麻布シティーホテル　　　　　　　　　　　(03) 3453-4311
Business H. Mate　ビジネスホテルメイツ　　　　　　　　(03) 3443-4161
Capitol Tōkyū H.　キャピトル東急ホテル　　　　　　　　(03) 3581-4511
Center H. Tokyo　センターホテル東京　　　　　　　　　　(03) 3667-2711 **71**
Central H.　セントラルホテル　　　　　　　　　　　　　(03) 3256-6251 **75**
Co-op Inn Shibuya　コープ・イン渋谷　　　　　　　　　　(03) 3486-6600
Diamond H.　ダイヤモンドホテル　　　　　　　　　　　　(03) 3263-2211 **40**
Fairmont H.　フェヤーモントホテル　　　　　　　　　　　(03) 3262-1151
Gajōen Kankō H.　雅叙園観光ホテル　　　　　　　　　　(03) 3491-0111
Ginza Capital H.　銀座キャピタルホテル　　　　　　　　(03) 3543-8211
Ginza Daiichi H.　銀座第一ホテル　　　　　　　　　　　(03) 3542-5311
Ginza International H.　銀座国際ホテル　　　　　　　　(03) 3574-1121 **68**
Ginza Marunouchi H.　銀座丸ノ内ホテル　　　　　　　　(03) 3543-5431
Ginza Nikkō H.　銀座日航ホテル　　　　　　　　　　　　(03) 3571-4911 **68**
Ginza Tōbu H.　銀座東武ホテル　　　　　　　　　　　　(03) 3546-0111 **69**
Ginza Tōkyū H.　銀座東急ホテル　　　　　　　　　　　　(03) 3541-2411 **69**
Goten-yama Hills H. Laforet Tokyo　　　　　　　　　　(03) 5488-3911 **59**
　御殿山ヒルズホテルラフォーレ東京
Grand Central H.　グランドセントラルホテル　　　　　　(03) 3256-3211 **75**
Haneda Tōkyū H.　羽田東急ホテル　　　　　　　　　　　(03) 3747-0311
Harumi Grand H.　晴海グランドホテル　　　　　　　　　(03) 3533-7111
Hill Port H.　ヒルポートホテル　　　　　　　　　　　　(03) 3462-5171
Hilltop (Yamanoue) H.　山の上ホテル　　　　　　　　　(03) 3293-2311 **74**
Hokke Club Tokyo (Ikenohata)　法華クラブ池之端店　　(03) 3822-3111
H. Juraku　ホテル聚楽　　　　　　　　　　　　　　　　(03) 3251-7222 **75**
Holiday Inn Tokyo　ホリデイ・イン東京　　　　　　　　(03) 3553-6161 **71**
H. Century Hyatt　ホテルセンチュリーハイアット　　　(03) 3349-0111 **38**
H. Edmont　ホテルエドモント　　　　　　　　　　　　　(03) 3237-1111 **41**
H. Friend　ホテルフレンド　　　　　　　　　　　　　　(03) 3866-2244
H. Ginza Dai-ei　ホテル銀座ダイエー　　　　　　　　　(03) 3541-2681
H. Grand Business　ホテルグランドビジネス　　　　　　(03) 3984-5121 **93**
H. Grand Palace　ホテルグランドパレス　　　　　　　　(03) 3264-1111 **41**
H. Hankyū　ホテル阪急　　　　　　　　　　　　　　　　(03) 3775-6121
H. Ibis　ホテルアイビス　　　　　　　　　　　　　　　(03) 3403-4411
H. Kayū Kaikan　ホテル霞友会館　　　　　　　　　　　(03) 3230-1111
H. Kizankan　ホテル機山館　　　　　　　　　　　　　　(03) 3812-1211
H. Dai-ei　ホテルダイエー　　　　　　　　　　　　　　(03) 3813-6271
H. Kokusai Kankō　ホテル国際観光　　　　　　　　　　(03) 3215-3281
H. Metropolitan　ホテルメトロポリタン　　　　　　　　(03) 3980-1111 **92**
H. Mita Kaikan　ホテル三田会館　　　　　　　　　　　(03) 3453-6601
H. New Meguro　ホテルニューメグロ　　　　　　　　　(03) 3719-8121
H. New Ōtani　ホテルニューオータニ　　　　　　　　　(03) 3265-1111 **64**
H. New Tokyo　ホテルニュー東京　　　　　　　　　　　(03) 3469-5211
H. Ōkura　ホテルオークラ　　　　　　　　　　　　　　(03) 3582-0111 **46**
H. Pacific Meridien Tokyo　ホテルパシフィック東京　　(03) 3445-6711 **58**
H. President Aoyama　ホテルプレジデント青山　　　　(03) 3497-0111 **45**
H. Satoh　ホテルサトー　　　　　　　　　　　　　　　(03) 3815-1133
H. Seaside Edogawa　ホテルシーサイド江戸川　　　　　(03) 3804-1180
H. Seiyō Ginza　ホテル西洋銀座　　　　　　　　　　　(03) 3585-1111

H. Sun City Ikebukuro　ホテルサンシティ池袋	(03) 3986-1101
H. Sunlite Sinjuku　ホテルサンライト新宿	(03) 3356-0391
H. Sunroute Shibuya　ホテルサンルート渋谷	(03) 3464-6411
H. Sunroute Tokyo　ホテルサンルート東京	(03) 3375-3211
H. Takanawa　ホテル高輪	(03) 5488-1000 ⓾
H. Tokyo　ホテル東京	(03) 3447-5771 ⓾
H. Tōkyū Kankō　ホテル東急観光	(03) 3582-0451 ㊻
H. Tōyō　ホテル東陽	(03) 3615-1041
H. Yaesu Ryūmeikan　ホテル八重洲竜名館	(03) 3271-0971 ⓰
H. Lungwood　ホテルラングウッド	(03) 3803-1234 ㊱
Ikebukuro H. Theatre　池袋ホテルテアトル	(03) 3988-2251 ㉝
Ikenohata Bunka Center　池之端文化センター	(03) 3822-0161
Imperial H. (Teikoku H.)　帝国ホテル	(03) 3504-1111 ⓲
Inabasō Ryokan　旅館稲葉荘	(03) 3341-9581
Kadoya H.　かどやホテル	(03) 3346-2561
Kayabachō Pearl H.　茅場町パールホテル	(03) 3553-2211
Keiō Plaza H.　京王プラザホテル	(03) 3344-0111 ⓱
Kichijōji Tōkyū Inn　吉祥寺東急イン	(0422) 47-0109
Kikuya Ryokan　喜久屋旅館	(03) 3841-6404
Marroad Inn Akasaka　マロウド・イン赤坂	(03) 3585-7611 ⓼
Mitsui Urban H. Ginza　三井アーバンホテル銀座	(03) 3572-4131 ⓲
Miyako H. Tokyo　都ホテル東京	(03) 3447-3111
Miyako Inn Tokyo　都イン東京	(03) 3454-3111 ⓾
New Central H.　ニューセントラルホテル	(03) 3256-2171
New Ōtani Inn Tokyo　ニューオータニイン東京	(03) 3779-9111
New Takanawa Prince H.　新高輪プリンスホテル	(03) 3442-1111 ⓾
Nihon Seinenkan H.　日本青年館ホテル	(03) 3401-0101
Ōmori Tōkyū Inn　大森東急イン	(03) 3768-0109
Palace H.　パレスホテル	(03) 3211-5211 ⓺
Roppongi Prince H.　六本木プリンスホテル	(03) 3587-1111 ㊻
Royal Park H.　ロイヤルパークホテル	(03) 3667-1111
Ryokan Katsutarō　旅館勝太郎	(03) 3821-9808 ㊱
Ryokan Mikawaya Bekkan　旅館三河屋別館	(03) 3843-2345 ⓴
Ryokan Okayasu　おかやす旅館	(03) 3452-5091
Ryokan Sansuisō　旅館山水荘	(03) 3441-7475
Ryōgoku Pearl H.　両国パールホテル	(03) 3626-3211
Ryōgoku River H.　両国リバーホテル	(03) 3634-1711
Satellite H. Kōrakuen　サテライトホテル後楽園	(03) 3814-0202
Sawanoya Ryokan　澤の屋旅館	(03) 3822-2251 ㉟
Shiba Park H.　芝パークホテル	(03) 3433-4141
Shibuya Business H.　渋谷ビジネスホテル	(03) 3409-9300 ⓼
Shibuya Tōbu H.　渋谷東武ホテル	(03) 3476-0111 ⓼
Shibuya Tōkyū Inn　渋谷東急イン	(03) 3498-0109 ⓼
Shinagawa Prince H.　品川プリンスホテル	(03) 3440-1111 ⓼
Shinbashi Dai-ichi H.　新橋第一ホテル	(03) 3501-4411 ⓲
Shinjuku New City H.　新宿ニューシティホテル	(03) 3375-6511
Shinjuku Park H.　新宿パークホテル	(03) 3356-0241 ⓸
Shinjuku Prince H.　新宿プリンスホテル	(03) 3205-1111 ⓼
Shinjuku Sunpark H.　新宿サンパークホテル	(03) 3362-7101
Shinjuku Washington H.　新宿ワシントンホテル	(03) 3343-3111 ⓱
Star H. Tokyo　スターホテル東京	(03) 3361-1111 ⓾

Suidōbashi Grand H.　水道橋グランドホテル	(03) 3816-2101
Suigetsu H./Ohgaisō　水月ホテル/鷗外荘	(03) 3822-4611 (36)
Sukeroku-no-yado Sadachiyo Bekkan　助六の宿　貞千代別館	(03) 3842-6431
Sunshine City Prince H.　サンシャインシティプリンスホテル	(03) 3988-1111 (93)
Taishō Central H.　大正セントラルホテル	(03) 3232-0101
Takanawa Prince H.　高輪プリンスホテル	(03) 3447-1111 (58)
Takanawa Tōbu H.　高輪東武ホテル	(03) 3447-0111 (58)
Takara H.　タカラホテル	(03) 3831-0101 (77)
Teikoku H. (Imperial H.)　帝国ホテル	(03) 3504-1111 (68)
Tōkō H.　東興ホテル	(03) 3494-1050
Tokyo Business H.　東京ビジネスホテル	(03) 3356-4605
Tokyo City H.　東京シティーホテル	(03) 3270-7671
Tokyo Grand H.　東京グランドホテル	(03) 3454-0311
Tokyo Green H. Awajichō　東京グリーンホテル淡路町	(03) 3255-4161 (75)
Tokyo Green H. Kōrakuen　東京グリーンホテル後楽園	(03) 3816-4161
Tokyo Green H. Suidōbashi　東京グリーンホテル水道橋	(03) 3295-4161
Tokyo Hilton International　東京ヒルトンインターナショナル	(03) 3344-5111 (90)
Tokyo H. Urashima　東京ホテル浦島	(03) 3533-3111 (54)
Tokyo Int'l Youth Hostel　東京国際ユースホステル	(03) 3235-1107
Tokyo Coma Ryokō Kaikan　東京コマ旅行会館	(03) 3585-1046 (83)
Tokyo Marunouchi H.　東京丸ノ内ホテル	(03) 3215-2151 (60)
Tokyo Prince H.　東京プリンスホテル	(03) 3432-1111 (53)
Tokyo Station H.　東京ステーションホテル	(03) 3231-2511 (61)
Tokyo Sunny Side H.　東京サニーサイドホテル	(03) 3649-1211
Tokyo YMCA H.　東京 YMCA ホテル	(03) 3293-1911
Tokyo YMCA Hostel　東京 YMCA ホステル	(03) 3293-5421
Tokyo YWCA Sadohara Hostel　東京 YWCA 砂土原ホステル	(03) 3268-7313
Toshi Center H.　都市センターホテル	(03) 3265-8211 (64)
Tsukuba H.　ツクバホテル	(03) 3834-2556
Ueno Terminal H.　上野ターミナルホテル	(03) 3831-1110 (77)
Yaesu Fujiya H.　八重洲富士屋ホテル	(03) 3273-2111 (61)
YMCA Asia Youth Center　YMCA アジア青少年センター	(03) 3233-0611

YOKOHAMA　横浜

Aster H.　アスターホテル	(045) 651-0141 (95)
Bund H.　バンドホテル	(045) 621-1101 (95)
Central Inn Yokohama　セントラルイン横浜	(045) 251-1010
Fuji View H. Shin-Yokohama　フジビューホテル新横浜	(045) 473-0021
Holiday Inn Yokohama　ホリデイ・イン横浜	(045) 681-3311 (95)
H. Empire　ホテルエンパイア	(045) 851-1431
H. New Grand　ホテルニューグランド	(045) 681-1841 (95)
H. Yokohama Garden　ホテル横浜ガーデン	(045) 641-1311
New Ōtani Inn Yokohama　ニューオータニイン横浜	(045) 252-1311
Satellite H. Yokohama　サテライトホテル横浜	(045) 641-0202 (95)
Shin-Yokohama Kokusai H.　新横浜国際ホテル	(045) 473-1311
Shin-Yokohama H.　新横浜ホテル	(045) 471-6011
Tsurumi Pearl H.　鶴見パールホテル	(045) 501-8080
Yokohama-Isezakichō Washington H.　横浜伊勢佐木町ワシントンホテル	(045) 243-7111
Yokohama Kokusai H.　横浜国際ホテル	(045) 311-1311
Yokohama Tōkyū H.　横浜東急ホテル	(045) 311-1682
Yokohama Prince H.　横浜プリンスホテル	(045) 751-1111

Tokyo Metropolitan Government　東京都庁(03)5321-1111　**91**

Ward Offices (City Offices)-*Kuyakusho* 区役所

Adachi　足立	(03)3882-1111 **31**		Nakano　中野	(03)3389-1111 **20**
Arakawa　荒川	(03)3802-3111 **31**		Nerima　練馬	(03)3993-1111 **20**
Bunkyō　文京	(03)3812-7111 **35**		Ōta　大田	(03)3773-5111 **25**
Chiyoda　千代田	(03)3264-0151 **41**		Setagaya　世田谷	(03)3412-1111 **23**
Chūō　中央	(03)3543-0211 **48**		Shibuya　渋谷	(03)3463-1211 **84**
Edogawa　江戸川	(03)3652-1151 **19**		Shinagawa　品川	(03)3777-1111 **39**
Itabashi　板橋	(03)3964-1111 **21**		Shinjuku　新宿	(03)3209-1111 **88**
Katsushika　葛飾	(03)3695-1111 **17**		Suginami　杉並	(03)3312-2111 **20**
Kita　北	(03)3908-1111 **21**		Sumida　墨田	(03)3626-3151 **18**
Kōtō　江東	(03)3647-9111 **18**		Taitō　台東	(03)3842-5311 **36**
Meguro　目黒	(03)3715-1111 **23**		Toshima　豊島	(03)3981-1111 **93**
Minato　港	(03)3578-2111 **53**			

City Offices-*Shiyakusho* 市役所

Akishima　昭島	(0425)44-5111 **12**		Kodaira　小平	(0423)41-1211 **10**
Akigawa　秋川	(0425)58-1111 **12**		Koganei　小金井	(0423)83-1111 **10**
Chōfu　調布	(0424)81-7111 **11**		Kokubunji　国分寺	(0423)25-0111 **10**
Fuchū　府中	(0423)64-4111 **10**		Komae　狛江	(03)3430-1111 **11**
Fussa　福生	(0425)51-1511 **12**		Kunitachi　国立	(0425)76-2111 **10**
Hachiōji　八王子	(0426)26-3111 **12**		Machida　町田	(0427)22-3111 **10**
Hamura　羽村	(0425)55-1111 **12**		Mitaka　三鷹	(0422)45-1151 **10**
Higashikurume　東久留米	(0424)73-5111 **10**		Musashimurayama　武蔵村山	(0425)65-1111 **10**
Higashimurayama　東村山	(0423)93-5111 **10**		Musashino　武蔵野	(0422)51-5131 **10**
Higashiyamato　東大和	(0425)63-2111 **10**		Ōme　青梅	(0428)22-1111
Hino　日野	(0425)85-1111 **10**		Tachikawa　立川	(0425)23-2111 **10**
Hōya　保谷	(0424)21-2525 **11**		Tama　多摩	(0423)75-8111 **10**
Inagi　稲城	(0423)78-2111 **11**		Tanashi　田無	(0424)64-1311 **10**
Kiyose　清瀬	(0424)92-5111 **10**			

Town Offices-*maciyakuba* 町役場

Hinode　日の出	(0425)97-0511		Mizuho　瑞穂	(0425)57-0501 **12**
Itsukaichi　五日市	(0425)96-1511 **12**		Okutama　奥多摩	(0428)83-2111

Oganizations　各種団体

AFS Japan Association, Inc.
エイ・エフ・エス日本協会　　　(03) 3591-5488
America-Japan Society, Inc.　日米協会
(03) 3201-0780
Amnesty Int'l Japanese Section
アムネスティ・インターナショナル日本支部
(03) 3203-1050
Asean Society　ASEAN協会　(03) 3230-0526
Asia Friendship Association
アジア親善交流協会　　　　　(03) 3580-7055
Asian Affairs Reserch Council　アジア調査会
(03) 3211-1616
Asia Center of Japan　アジア会館
(03) 3402-6111
Asian Club　アジアクラブ　　(03) 3435-6071
Asian Culture Center for UNESCO (ACCU)　ユ
ネスコ・アジア文化センター　(03) 3269-4435
Association of Int'l Education, Japan
日本国際教育協会　　　　　　(03) 3467-3521
Association for Japanese-Language Teaching
国際日本語普及協会　　　　　(03) 3400-9031
Association for Overseas Technical Scholaship
海外技術者研修協会　　　　　(03) 3888-8211
Association for Promotion of Int'l Cooperation
国際協力推進協会　　　　　　(03) 3504-2085
Australia-Japan Foundation　豪日交流基金
(03) 3498-4141
Broadcast Programming of Japan
放送番組センター　　　　　　(03) 3264-3641
Canada-Japan Society　日加協会
(03) 3581-0925
Center for Int'l Cultural Studies & Education
(ICS)　国際文化教育センター　(03) 3567-4681
Center for Int'l Students in Japan
在日留学生交流センター　　　(03) 3354-6637
English Language Education Council, Inc.
英語教育協議会　　　　　　　(03) 3265-8911
Foundation of International Education
国際教育協会　　　　　　　　(03) 3437-6591
Foundation of International Education
国際教育財団　　　　　　　　(03) 3449-7045
Foundation for Int'l Information Processing
Eduacation　情報処理教育研修助成財団
(03) 3215-2240

Friendship Force of Japan　世界友情協会
(03) 3564-0249
Goethe Institute, German Cultural Center
東京ドイツ文化センター　　　(03) 3584-3201
Group Work Association for Youth
勤労青少年グループ協会　　　(03) 3508-2048
Hitachi Scholaship Foundation
日立国際奨学財団　　　　　　(03) 3258-1111
Honda Foundation　本田財団　(03) 3274-5125
Hoso Bunka Foundation　放送文化基金
(03) 3464-3131
Institute of Eastern Culture　東方学会
(03) 3261-1061
Institute for Language Experience, Experiment
& Exchange　言語交流研究所 (03) 3467-6151
Int'l Society for Educational Information, Tokyo
Inc. Institute for the Checking of Textbooks &
Educational Materials
国際教育情報センター教科書、教育資料調査
研究所　　　　　　　　　　　(03) 3358-1138
International Artists Center
国際芸術家センター　　　　　(03) 3582-9171
International Education Center
国際教育振興会　　　　　　　(03) 3359-9621
International Friendship Association
インターナショナル・フレンドシップ・アソシ
エーション　　　　　　　　　(03) 3463-4946
Int'l Friendship Culture Association
国際親善文化協会　　　　　　(03) 3466-3028
Int'l Hospitality & Conference Service Association
国際交流サービス協会　　　　(03) 3580-1621
International Internship Programs
インターナショナル・インターンシップ・プロ
グラムズ　　　　　　　　　　(03) 3787-1973
Int'l Pen Friends Society
国際ペン・フレンド協会　　　(03) 3155-4322
Internaional Students Institute　国際学友会
(03) 3371-7265
Int'l Youth Association of Japan　国際青少年研
修協会　　　　　　　　　　　(03) 3572-3351
Inter-university Seminar-House
大学セミナーハウス　　　　　(0426) 76-8511
Ishizaka Foundation　石坂記念財団

(03) 3279-1411

Iwatani Naoji Foundation　岩谷直治記念財団
(03) 3580-2251

Japan External Trade Organization (JETRO)
日本貿易振興会　　　　　　(03) 3582-5511

Japan Film Library Council (Kawakita Memorial
Film Institute)　川喜多記念映画文化財団
(03) 3561-6719

Japan Indonesia Association, Inc.
日本インドネシア協会　　(03) 3661-2956

Japan Institute for Social & Economic Affairs
経済広報センター　　　　　(03) 3201-1411

Japan International Artist Club
ジャパン・インターナショナル・アーティス
ト・クラブ　　　　　　　　(03) 3463-4946

Japan Int'l Friendship Center Int'l 3F Club
日本国際親善センター　　(03) 3353-1673

Japan-Iran Society　日本イラン協会
(03) 3356-5537

Japan Library Association　日本図書館協会
(03) 3410-6411

Japan-Malaysia Association
日本マレイシア協会　　　　(03) 3989-1233

Japan Micronesia Association
日本ミクロネシア協会　　(03) 3403-8474

Japan Municipal League for Int'l Friendship
国際親善都市連盟　　　　　(03) 3262-5231

Japan National Tourist Organization
国際観光振興会　　　　　　(03) 3216-1901

Japan Office, The U.S.-Japan Culture Center
日米文化センター日本事務所　(03) 3353-2431

Japan Overseas Cooperation ex-Volunteers
Association　青年海外協力隊 OB 会
(03) 3400-7261

Japan Overseas Educational Services
海外子女教育振興財団　　(03) 3580-2521

Japan-American Cultural Society
日米文化振興会　　　　　　(03) 3237-9541

Japanese Association of the Experiment in Int'
l Living　日本国際生活体験協会　(03) 3261-3451

Japan Audio-Visual Education Association
日本視聴覚教育協会　　　　(03) 3591-2186

Japan Australia Society　日濠協会
(03) 3457-1471

Japan-British Society　日英協会　(03) 3211-8027

Japan Center for Int'l Exchange
日本国際交流センター　　(03) 3446-7781

Japan-China Cultural Exchange Association
日本中国文化交流協会　　(03) 3212-1766

Japan China Friendship Association
日本中国友好協会　　　　　(03) 3291-4231

Japan-China Society　日中協会　(03) 3583-6818

Japan Cultural Association with Foreign Coun-
tries　日本対外文化協会　(03) 3407-4536

Japan Economic Research Center
日本経済研究センター　　(03) 3270-5541

Japan Economic Reserch Institute
日本経済調査協議会　　　　(03) 3214-0541

Japanese Center of the I.T.I
国際演劇協会日本センター　(03) 3478-7881

Japan Pen Club　日本ペンクラブ
(03) 3402-1171

Japan Securities Scholaship Foundation
日本証券奨学財団　　　　　(03) 3664-7113

Japan Society for the Promotion of Science
日本学術振興会　　　　　　(03) 3263-1721

Japan Solidarity Committee for Asian Alumni
アジア留学生協力会　　　　(03) 3404-0690

Japan Spanish Society　日本スペイン協会
(03) 3353-0428

Japan Thailand Association　日本タイ協会
(03) 3241-2838

Japan-United States Educational Commission
日米教育委員会　　　　　　(03) 3580-3231

Japan-United States Friendship Commission
日米友好基金　　　　　　　(03) 3508-2380

Kajima Foundation for the Arts　鹿島美術財団
(03) 3582-5920

Kanagawa Int'l Association
神奈川県国際交流協会　　(045) 671-7070

Kazankai　霞山会　　　　(03) 3581-0401

Korean Cultural Service　韓国文化院
(03) 3988-9271

Korean YMCA in Japan Asia Youth Center
在日本韓国 YMCA アジア青少年センター
(03) 3233-0611

Labo Int'l Exchange Foundation
ラボ国際交流財団　　　　　(03) 3367-2431

Matsushita Audio Visual Education Foundation
松下視聴覚教育研究財団　(03) 3431-6363

Mitsubishi Bank Foundationn
三菱銀行国際財団　　　　　(03) 3240-3337

Moriya Foundation　守屋学生交流協会
(03) 3263-7952

National Assembly for Youth Development
青少年育成国民会議　　　　(03) 3460-4151

National Council of Youth Organizations in
Japan

中央青少年団体連絡協議会　　(03) 3470-2271

NHK, International Incorporated
　NHK インターナショナル　　(03) 3464-1823

Nippon Association for Education 2001 (NAFE)
　21世紀教育の会　　(03) 3479-3921

Nippon Clultural Center　日本文化財団
　　　　　　　　　　　　(03) 3580-0031

Nippon Television Network Cultural Society
　日本テレビ放送網文化事業団　(03) 3261-9612

Pacific Educational and Cultural Exchange
　(peace)
　太平洋教育文化交流協会　　(03) 3496-3501

Publishers Association for Cultural Exchange,
　Japan
　出版文化国際交流会　　(03) 3291-5685

Rotary Yoneyama Memorial Foundation
　ロータリー米山記念奨学会　(03) 3434-8681

Saneyoshi Scholarship Foundation
　実吉奨学会　　(03) 3241-2907

Sankei Scholarship Foundation
　サンケイスカラシップ　　(03) 3279-4420

Sanwa Bank Foundation　三和国際基金
　　　　　　　　　　　　(03) 3211-7870

Science and Technology Foundation of Japan
　国際科学技術財団　　(03) 3508-7691

Southeast Asian Friendship & Culture Associa-
　tion
　東南アジア文化友好協会　　(03) 3985-1967

The Africa Society of Japan　アフリカ協会
　　　　　　　　　　　　(03) 3501-1878

The Asia Foundation　アジア財団
　　　　　　　　　　　　(03) 3441-8291

The Asian Students Cultural Association　アジ
　ア学生文化協会　　(03) 3946-4121

The British Council, Japan
　ブリティッシュ・カウンシル　(03) 3264-3721

The Centre for East Asian Cultural Studies
　ユネスコ東アジア文化研究センター
　　　　　　　　　　　　(03) 3942-0121

The Eastern Institute,Inc.　東方研究会
　　　　　　　　　　　　(03) 3251-4081

The Indo-Japanese Association　日印協会
　　　　　　　　　　　　(03) 3271-9476

The International House of Japan,Inc.
　国際文化会館　　(03) 3470-4611

The Japanese Red Cross Society
　日本赤十字社　　(03) 3438-1311

The Japan Foundation　国際交流基金
　　　　　　　　　　　　(03) 3263-4491

The Japan Institute of Int'l Affairs (JILIA)
　日本国際問題研究所　　(03) 3503-7261

The Japan Singapore Association
　日本シンガポール協会　　(03) 3403-3719

The Matsumae Int'l Foundation
　松前国際友好財団　　(03) 3581-1070

The Middle East Institute of Japan　中東調査会
　　　　　　　　　　　　(03) 3591-0955

The Naito Foundation　内藤記念科学振興財団
　　　　　　　　　　　　(03) 3813-3005

The Overseas Japanese Association
　海外日系人協会　　(03) 3262-0260

The Society for Teaching Japanese as a Foreign
　Language　日本語教育学会 (03) 3584-4872

The Toyota Foundation　トヨタ財団
　　　　　　　　　　　　(03) 3344-1701

Tokyo American Center, United States Informa-
　tion Service U.S. Embassy, Tokyo
　米国大使館広報・文化交流局・東京アメリカン
　センター　　(03) 3436-0904

Tokyo Young Women's Christian Association
　東京基督教女子青年会　　(03) 3293-5421

Tokyu Foundation for Inbound Students
　とうきゅう外来留学生奨学財団 (03) 3461-0844

Unesco Art Education League in Japan
　ユネスコ美術教育連盟　　(03) 3463-4946

Unijapan Film Asso. for thc Diffusion of
　Japanese Film Abroad
　日本映画海外普及協会　　(03) 3572-5106

United States-Japan Foundation　米日財団
　　　　　　　　　　　　(03) 3591-4002

World Youth Exchange Association
　世界青少年交流協会　　(03) 3262-6301

Yokohama Association for Int'l Communica-
　tions & Exchanges
　横浜市海外交流協会　　(045) 671-7128

Yoshida Foundation for Science and Technol-
　ogy
　吉田科学技術財団　　(03) 3263-4916

Yoshida Int'l Education Foundation
　吉田国際教育基金　　(03) 3271-1051

Youth for Understanding, Japan
　YFU 日本協会　　(03) 3406-0141

Useful Phrases　道のたずね方

Please point out where I am on this map ?
この地図でここはどこですか？
Kono chizu de koko wa, doko desu ka?

What street is this ?
ここは何通りですか？
Koko wa, nani dōri desu ka?

Please show me where the —— station is?
—— 駅はどこですか？
—— Eki wa, doko desu ka ?

bus stop	subway	post office	bank
バス停	地下鉄	郵便局	銀行
basu-tei	chikatetsu	yūbinkyoku	ginkō

entrance	eixt	museum
入口	出口	博物館
iriguchi	deguchi	hakubutsu-kan

Where is the restroom ?
お手洗いはどこですか？
Otearai wa, doko desu ka ?

Where is the lavatory ?
トイレはどこですか？
Toire wa, doko desu ka ?

Where do I get off to go to the —— art museum ?
—— 美術館に行くには、どこで降りればいいですか？
—— bijutsu-kan ni ikuni wa, doko de orire-ba iidesu ka ?

Does this bus go to Ginza ?
このバスは銀座まで行きますか？
Kono basu wa, Ginza made ikimasu ka ?

Where is the ticket window ?
キップ売場はどこですか？
Kippu uriba wa, doko desu ka ?

What time does it leave ?
それは何時に出ますか？
Sore wa, nanji ni demasu ka ?

How long will it take ?
どのくらいかかりますか？
Dono kurai kakari masu ka ?

Do I have to change ?
のりかえが必要ですか？
Norikae ga hitsuyō desu ka ?

The Teikoku Hotel, please.
帝国ホテルまで行ってください。
Teikoku hoteru made itte kudasai.

I get off here.
ここでおります。
Koko de ori masu.

How much is it ?
いくらですか？
Ikura desu ka ?

東京2カ国語マップ　TOKYO MAP

1993年 3 月15日	第 1 刷発行　定価1,100円(本体1,068円)	
編　者	㈱アイリス社	
発行者	渡邊周一	
	遠藤　茂	
発行所	柏美術出版株式会社	
	東京都文京区向丘 1 -10- 2 -204A (〒113)　電話 03(3812)5136	
発　売	柏書房株式会社	
	東京都文京区本駒込 1 -13-14 (〒113)　電話 03(3947)8251	
製　版	エル工房　印刷・製本 凸版印刷㈱	ISBN 4 -7601-0877- 7

Routes to Airports
空港への交通路

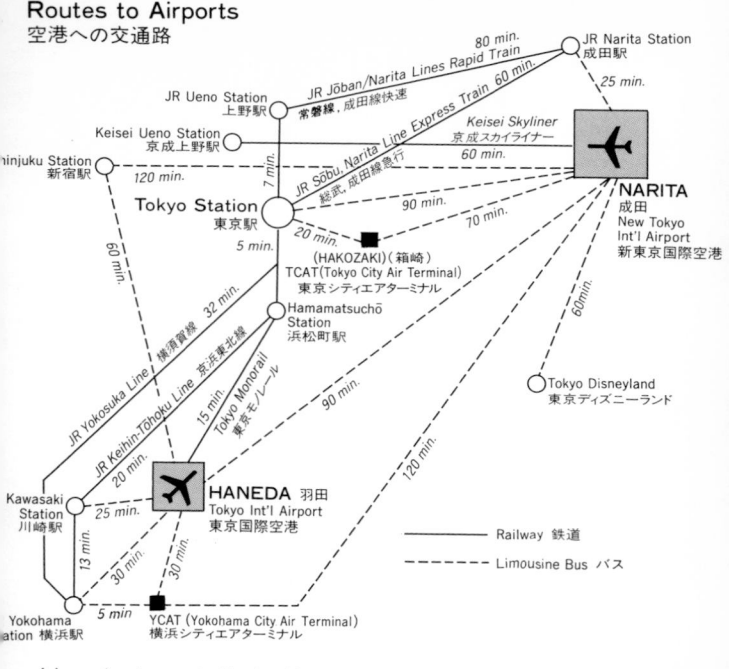

JR Narita Station 成田駅

JR Jōban/Narita Lines Rapid Train 80 min. 常磐線、成田線快速

JR Ueno Station 上野駅

Keisei Ueno Station 京成上野駅

25 min.

JR Jōban/Narita Lines Express Train 60 min.

Keisei Skyliner 京成スカイライナー 60 min.

Shinjuku Station 新宿駅

120 min.

7 min.

JR Sōbu, Narita Line 総武、成田線急行

Tokyo Station 東京駅

90 min.

70 min.

NARITA 成田 New Tokyo Int'l Airport 新東京国際空港

20 min.

5 min.

(HAKOZAKI)(箱崎) TCAT(Tokyo City Air Terminal) 東京シティエアーミナル

60 min.

60 min.

Hamamatsuchō Station 浜松町駅

JR Yokosuka Line / 横須賀線 32 min.

JR Keihin-Tōhoku Line 京浜東北線

Tokyo Monorail 東京モノレール 15 min.

Tokyo Disneyland 東京ディズニーランド

90 min.

20 min.

HANEDA 羽田 Tokyo Int'l Airport 東京国際空港

Kawasaki Station 川崎駅

25 min.

13 min.

30 min.

30 min.

120 min.

Railway 鉄道

Limousine Bus バス

Yokohama Station 横浜駅

5 min.

YCAT (Yokohama City Air Terminal) 横浜シティエアターミナル

Limousine buses to Narita Airport are also available at the following hotels:
リムジンバス発着ホテル

Akasaka Prince	赤坂プリンス ⑥	New Ōtani	ニューオータニ ⑥
Akasaka Tōkyū	赤坂東急 ⑥	New TakanaWa Prince	新高輪プリンス
ANA H. Tokyo	東京全日空 ⑧	Ōkura	オークラ ⑯
Century Hyatt	センチュリー ハイアット	Pacific Meridian Tokyo	パシフィック東京 ⑱
Daiichi Tokyo Bay	第一東京ベイ	Palace	パレス ⑫
Ginza Tōbu	銀座東武 ⑥	Sheraton	シェラトン
Ginza Tōkyū	銀座東急 ⑥	Shinbashi Dai-Ichi	新橋第一 ⑱
Grand Palace	グランドパレス ㊶	Shinjuku Washington	新宿ワシントン ⑨
Haneda Tōkyū	羽田東急	Sunroute	サンルート
Hilton	ヒルトン	Sunshine City Prince	
Keiō Plaza	京王プラザ ⑨		サンシャインシティープリンス ㊙
Imperial (Teikoku)	帝国 ⑱	Takanawa Prince	高輪プリンス
Metropolitan	メトロポリタン ⑨	Tokyo Hilton Int'l	東京ヒルトンインターナショナル ⑨
Miyako	都	Tokyo Prince	東京プリンス ㊺

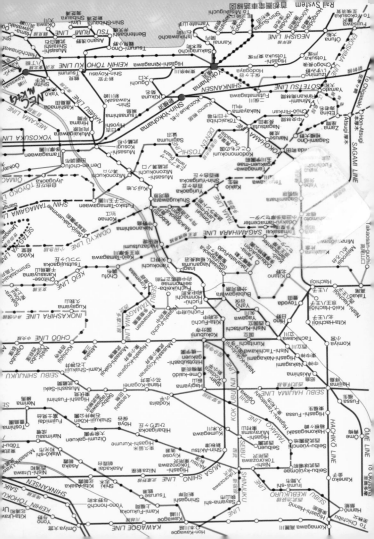